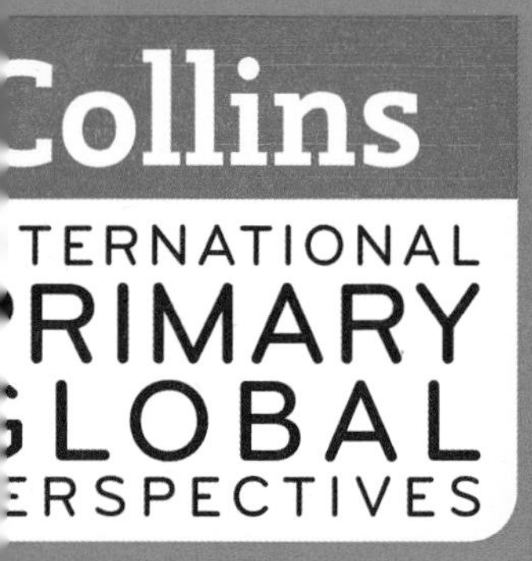

Student's Book 3

William Collins' dream of knowledge for all began with the publication of his first book in 1819.

A self-educated mill worker, he not only enriched millions of lives, but also founded a flourishing publishing house. Today, staying true to this spirit, Collins books are packed with inspiration, innovation and practical expertise.

They place you at the centre of a world of possibility and give you exactly what you need to explore it.

Collins. Freedom to teach.

Published by Collins

An imprint of HarperCollins*Publishers*
The News Building, 1 London Bridge Street, London, SE1 9GF, UK

HarperCollins*Publishers*
Macken House, 39/40 Mayor Street Upper, Dublin 1 D01 C9W8

Browse the complete Collins catalogue at **collins.co.uk**

10 9 8 7 6 5 4 3 2 1

ISBN 978-0-00-854958-9

British Library Cataloguing-in-Publication Data
A catalogue record for this publication is available from the British Library.

Series editor: Nick Coates
Author: Rebecca Adlard
Publisher: Elaine Higgleton
Product developer: Roisin Leahy
Development editor: Sonya Newland
Copyeditor: Catherine Dakin
Proofreader: Gudrun Kaiser
Illustrations: Jouve India Ltd.
Cover designer: Gordon MacGilp
Typesetter: David Jimenez, Ken Vail Graphic Design
Production controller: Lyndsey Rogers
Printed and bound in Italy by Grafica Veneta S.p.a

We are grateful to MInal Mistry for providing feedback on the Student's Book as it was developed.

This book is produced from independently certified FSC™ paper to ensure responsible forest management.

For more information visit: harpercollins.co.uk/green

Contents

Introduction: How to use this book v
Unit 1: We can build it! 1
1.1 How do we work together? 2
1.2 What are you good at? 4
1.3 Who makes a building? 6
1.4 Who else works on a new building? 8
1.5 What's your idea? 10
1.6 What would we like to build where we live? 12
Unit 1 Final task: Design and build a structure 14
Reflection: How successful was our building task? 16
Unit 2: Rule Makers 17
2.1 What are the rules about friendship? 18
2.2 How similar are we? 20
2.3 Playing the game 22
2.4 How many rules does our school have? 24
2.5 I have some questions 26
2.6 Can I ask you some questions? 28
Unit 2 Final task: Create a school rules questionnaire 30
Reflection: How successful was our school rules questionnaire? 32
Unit 3: Older and wiser 33
3.1 What is young? What is old? 34
3.2 How many older people are there in Australia? 37
3.3 What do older people do? 40
3.4 What's important to older people? 42

3.5 What do we know and think about older people? 44
3.6 How can we make an age-friendly community? 46
Unit 3 Final task: Plan an age-friendly community 48
Reflection: How successful was our age-friendly community plan? 50
Unit 4: A fair life! 51
4.1 What does 'fair' mean? 52
4.2 What do you need? 54
4.3 What is fair trade? 56
4.4 What fair trade foods can we buy? 58
4.5 The journey 60
4.6 Do you agree about fair trade? 62
Unit 4 Final task: Create a letter or video about fair trade 64
Reflection: How successful was our letter or video? 66
Unit 5: You are welcome! 67
5.1 Where do our families come from? 68
5.2 What is migration? 70
5.3 What is different about our countries? 72
5.4 What is your family heritage? 75
5.5 What is it like starting at a new school? 76
5.6 What is great about living here? 78
Unit 5 Final task: Make a welcome video 80
Reflection: How successful was our welcome video? 82
Glossary of key terms 83
Acknowledgements 84

How to use this book

Use this book in your lessons, to learn about a range of global topics!

The skills box shows you the main and subsidiary skills that you will learn and practise in this lesson.

✓ **Main**
✓ Subsidiary

Key terms

Key terms are important words or phrases that will help you understand what to do in each lesson.

Useful language

The useful phrases and sentences provided will help you discuss the topic ...

- An activity that involves reading
- An activity that involves listening
- An activity that involves working in a pair
- An activity that involves working in a group

Talking point:

- You will look back on what you have learned in the lesson, and talk about things that went well with your classmates.

Before you go:

- Think about how you will use your new skills!

Unit 1 We can build it!

What do you know?

- What can you see in the photos?
- Are the people working on their own or in teams?

In this unit, you will:

- Think about why and how we work in teams.
- Write a questionnaire.
- Look at ways to record information.

1.1 How do we work together?

✓ Reflection
✓ Collaboration

1. Play 'Capture the Castle'. Your teacher will tell you the rules.

2. Do you like playing games in teams? Take a class survey.

3. Look at the picture. Explain what it means.

4. Why is it sometimes difficult to work in a team?

Key term

survey: a way to find out information from a lot of different people by asking them all the same question

Useful language

I think it means …

It might mean that …

It shows the idea that …

Do the quiz.

When you work in a team ...

	A	B
1 You should:	Contribute ideas.	Let other people contribute all the ideas.
2 You should:	Listen to other people's ideas.	Try not to listen to other people's ideas.
3 You should:	Choose the best ideas and use them.	Choose the best parts of all the different ideas and put them together.
4 Who decides?	The team should choose the best idea together.	The cleverest person in the team should choose which idea to do.
5 You should always:	Help others in the group.	Focus on what you need to do and not help others with their tasks.
6 If you do not know what to do:	You must work it out.	You must ask for help.
7 You should stop when:	You have done your part of the task.	The task is completely finished.

Talking point

Did the activities in this lesson help you to think about how to work well in a team? How?

How confident do you feel about working in a team? Choose green (very confident), amber (getting there) or red (not very confident).

Before you go

What must we remember to do when we work in a team?

1.2 What are you good at?

✓ **Communication**
✓ Reflection

1 **Find the speakers in the picture.**

I'm good at photography. I'm a camera operator.

I'm good at computers. I'm a sound engineer.

I enjoy acting. I'm an actor.

I'm good at making decisions and giving instructions. I'm a director.

2 **Read the talking partners checklist.**

Checklist

Talking partners

✓ Sit facing your partner.
✓ Take turns to speak.
✓ Look at your partner when you are talking together.
✓ Listen to what your partner is saying.
✓ Show interest by nodding your head, smiling or responding.

3 Let's practise! Tell your partner what you are good at.

4 Join up with another pair. Use the talking partners checklist to help them improve.

5 Ask your partner a question.

Useful language

I'm good at … I'm not good at …

I enjoy …

I don't enjoy …

I like … but I prefer …

Talking point

Which of the jobs in Activity 1 would you like best? Why?

How good do you think you and your partner were at talking together today? Choose gold, silver or bronze.

Before you go

Did the activities today help you to understand what you are good at or what you enjoy doing? Why do you think it is important to understand these things?

1.3 Who makes a building?

✓ **Collaboration**
✓ Research
✓ Communication

1 **Look at the picture in the city below. What can you see? Does it look the same as or different from where you live?**

2 **Read the title. What is the text about?**

3 **Read the text. Answer the questions.**

a Is this a story or an information text?

b What is the Burj Khalifa?

c What shape is the Burj Al-Arab?

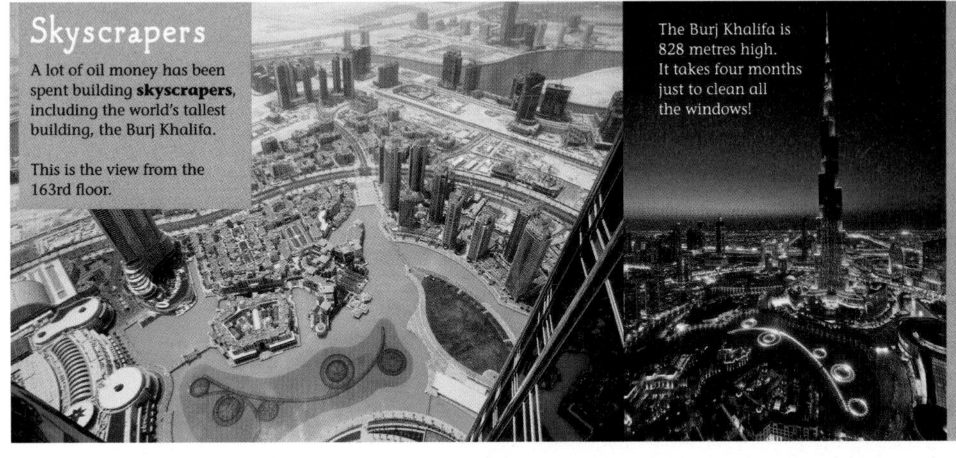

Dubai's first skyscraper was built in 1979. It now has more skyscrapers than any other city.

The Burj Al-Arab is a hotel, shaped like the sail of a trading boat from old Dubai.

4 **Read the messages. Answer the questions.**

a What two jobs can you find?

b What building did both men work on?

Hi! I'm Rami. I'm an architect. I helped to design the Burj Khalifa.

Hi! I'm Andreas. I'm an engineer. I made sure the Burj Khalifa won't fall down.

We worked together to make the Burj Khalifa.

5 Read the 'Doing partners' checklist. Then, be engineers and architects. Use the worksheets.

Checklist

Doing partners

- ✓ Read the instructions together.
- ✓ Take turns to speak.
- ✓ Listen to what your partner is saying and respond nicely.
- ✓ Agree on who will do what.
- ✓ Share materials.
- ✓ Explain what you are doing as you do it.

Useful language

Let's …

We could …

Why don't I do … and you do …?

What do you think? Do you agree? Do you have a better idea?

6 Present your new skyscraper to another pair.

Useful language

We'd like to show you our idea for a new … /This is our skyscraper.

It's made from … It's very … It's in the shape of a … /It's a … shape.

We decided on this design because …

The part we like most about our design is …

I'm sorry, could you repeat that please?

Talking point

Use the 'Doing partners' checklist to answer these questions:

- Did you suggest ideas for the tasks today?
- Did you work well with your partner?

How good were you and your doing partner at working together today? Choose.

Before you go

Did you learn anything new today about who makes a building? What was it?

1.4 Who else works on a new building?

✓ **Collaboration**
✓ Research

1 Find your building team.

- Read the card your teacher gives you.
- Walk around and ask others what they do in the building team.
- Tell them what you do.
- Find five other people with different roles and make a building team.

2 Complete the table on the worksheet.

3 Which job would you like most? Why?

4 Read the task. What does the team need to make?

Useful language

I'd like this job because it's …
I'm good at/interested in …
I enjoy … /I know a lot about …

In your group, you are going to make a bridge. You can only use paper, string and sticky tape. Your bridge must hold the weight of 10 coins.

5 **The team has decided on the following roles. Match the speech bubbles to who might say them.**

Manager
Makes sure that everyone listens to everyone else and that everyone is on task.
Errand runner
Makes a list of materials needed and gets them. Returns materials at the end of the task. Goes to the teacher with any questions the team has.
Recorder and presenter
Records the work by taking photos and making notes. Presents the outcome to the teacher or to the class.
Builder
Follows the team plan to make the bridge. Tells the errand runner what materials they need and if they have questions for the teacher.

1
How shall we start?
Does this look right?
Should we change it to make it better?
Can you get some more … please?

2
What shall we say about …?
Shall we show/say …?

3
Ideas, please.
Would you like to say something?
Let's hear from …
That's interesting.
Let's get on with the next step now.
Good work!

4
I'll get some more …
What else do we need?
Do you think we should ask the teacher?

6 **Imagine that your group is going to build the bridge. What role would you each do? Why?**

Talking point

Why might it be good to do your favourite role in a group task? Do you think it's important that you always do your favourite role in a group task? What do you think is the most important thing to remember when you work in a team?

Before you go

Did you learn anything new today about other people who are involved in making a new building?

1.5 What's your idea?

✓ **Collaboration**
✓ Reflection

1 **What task was the group going to do in? What materials were they allowed to use?**

2 **Now you are going to do the task. What types of bridges do you know?**

3 **Draw an idea for a bridge made of paper.**

4 **In Noemi's group, one person wants to be the manager and the rest of the group want to be builders. What can they do?**

5 Decide who will do what in your group.

manager | errand runner | recorder and presenter | builder

6 Make your bridge.

Checklist

Build a bridge!

✓ Listen to everyone's ideas.
✓ Vote for the best idea or take the best bits to make the best possible bridge.
✓ Make a list of materials you need.
✓ Make the bridge.
✓ Take photos or notes of what you are doing.
✓ Test your bridge!

7 How helpful were you to your group today? Copy and colour in the stars to show what you think.

Talking point

Was today's task easy or difficult? Why?

Did you like the role you did in today's task? Would you like to try a different role next time? Which one and why?

Before you go

How useful were your ideas today? Did they help the team?

1.6 What would we like to build where we live?

✓ **Research**
✓ Communication

1 Play I-Spy. Use the worksheet.

2 What buildings do you like in your town or region? Tell your class about one of them.

3 Draw and label a building you like. Give your picture a title.

4 Describe your picture to a partner.

5 Imagine that you are a developer. What building would you like to build in your town or region? Why? Write down your ideas.

6 Share your ideas in groups. Remember to take turns to speak and ask questions.

Useful language

That's a great idea!

That's really interesting!

What a good suggestion!

Talking point

Did you enjoy the activities in today's lesson? What suggestions for new buildings or structures did you like best? How well did your group share their ideas?

Before you go

Did you find out anything new about where you live?

Unit 1 Final task: Design and build a structure

✓ **Collaboration**
✓ Communication
✓ Reflection

Read the final task and discuss the questions.

Work in a team of five or six people. Agree on **a building you would like to build** in your town or region. Think about **where** you would build it. As a team, **design and build a model** of the building or structure using recycled materials. You should **decide who will do what job** in the task.

1. **How will you complete this task successfully? Use the words in bold, in the box above, to help you.**

2. **Discuss what building or structure you would like to build. You could use some of the ideas from Lesson 1.6, on page 12, or think of a different type of building or structure. What about:**

a library

a museum

a police station

a theatre

a supermarket

a school

a post office

a factory

3 Complete a group plan.

a Decide who will do what role in your group. Do you need:

- a recorder
- a manager
- a designer
- an errand runner
- a builder?

The recorder should write your roles in the table on the worksheet.

b Discuss what materials you will use to build your structures. On the worksheet, record what you are going to build, why and what materials you will use.

4 Make your model. Use the 'Top tips' to help you.

5 Present your model to the class. Tell your audience:

- what you have built
- why you chose it
- where you would build it
- what the model is made of
- what the real building would be made of.

Top tips

- Use previous lessons in this unit to help you work well in your group.
- Use the words in bold in the task box to help you do the task well.
- Be a good team member.
- Ask your teacher if you have questions.

Reflection: How successful was our building task?

a Complete the final task checklist. Use the worksheet and answer the questions.

Final task checklist			
Our model shows what we would like to build in our town or region.	☺	😐	☹
In our group, we all had clear jobs to do and we did them.	☺	😐	☹
Everyone in our group made suggestions.	☺	😐	☹

b Share your checklist with your team. Do you all agree?

c Take turns to say what you did to help the team. Do you all agree?

Before you go

Discuss these questions with your talking partner.

Who did you work with in your group?

Can you say one thing each person did that helped to get the job done?

Was it easier to do this task in a group than on your own?

Did you need any help during the task? If yes, who did you ask?

What did you enjoy most about working with this group?

Unit 2 Rule makers

What do you know?

- What does the sign tell us?
- What other swimming-pool rules do you know?

In this unit, you will:

- Talk about rules you know and why we have them.
- Write a research question and a questionnaire.
- Look at ways to record information.

2.1 What are the rules about friendship?

✓ **Communication**
✓ Research

1 **Kai and Nimalan are in different countries. What topic are they talking about?**

Hi, Nimalan, I'm Kai. Let's talk about friends. My group has made a list of friendship rules we think are important. Do you and your friends have the same rules?

Hi Kai. Thanks! Please read our ideas about being friends. Do we think differently about friendship?

2 **Read the two lists of friendship rules. Which of their ideas are the same and which are different?**

Our rules for friendship groups

1) A friendship group should have four or five people in it.
2) If you are in a friendship group or have a best friend, you should always play with them and not with others.
3) Friends share your interests and hobbies, and they like what you like.
4) Think of friends first. Friends are important.
5) You shouldn't keep secrets from a friend.
6) You shouldn't talk about a friend if they aren't there.
7) You shouldn't stay angry with a friend.

by Kai's group

Our ideas about friendship

1) Good friends play with each other and with anyone else they want to.
2) Friends need time apart, other friends and different hobbies.
3) Friends may argue and disagree, but they always talk about why they were sad.
4) Friends try to understand each other, forgive each other and stay friends.
5) Friends never say mean things about each other to other people.
6) Friends are special.

by Nimalan's group

3 Copy and complete this Venn diagram.

Key terms

Venn diagram: a way to show where two things are similar and where they are different

Kai	Both	Nimalan
Friends don't keep secrets from each other	Friends are important	Friends don't always have to play or spend time together

4 Which ideas about friendship do you prefer, Kai's or Nimalan's?

5 Discuss your own ideas and rules about friendship.

6 Make a poster of the friendship rules you all agree on.

Useful language

I think that … because …

Do you agree? What do you think?

I don't agree because in my opinion …

What do we all agree on?

Talking point

Did you enjoy working in your group today? Were you a good group member? Why or why not?

Before you go

Is it helpful to have friendship rules?

2.2 How similar are we?

✓ **Communication**
✓ Research

1 **Trace your hand. Write five things about yourself. Use the worksheet.**

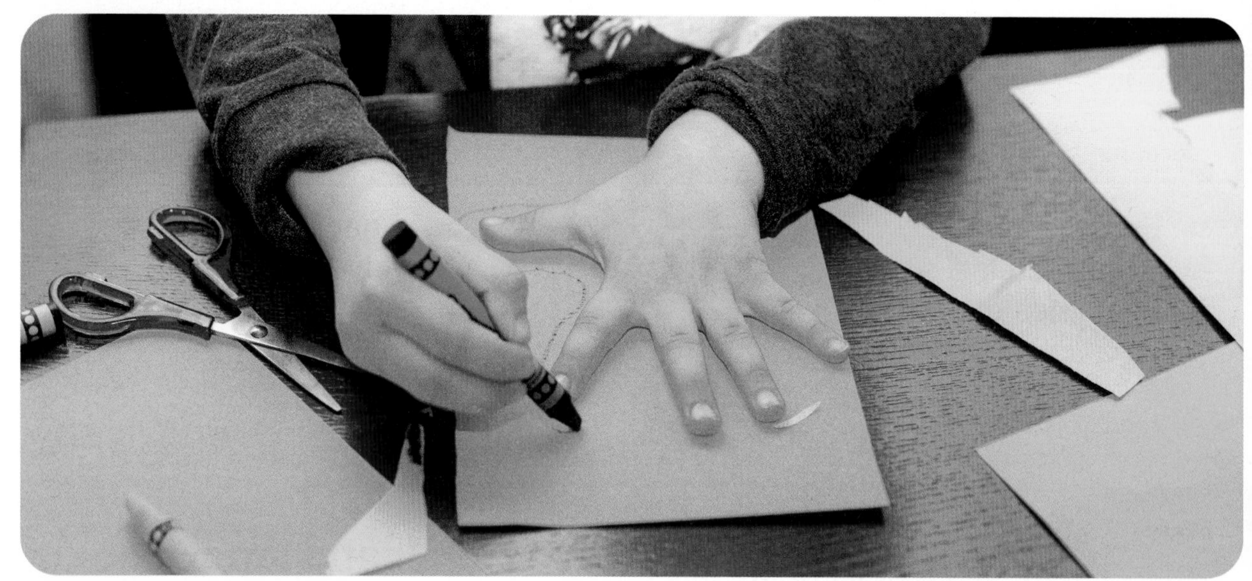

2 **Copy and complete the Venn diagram about you your partner.**

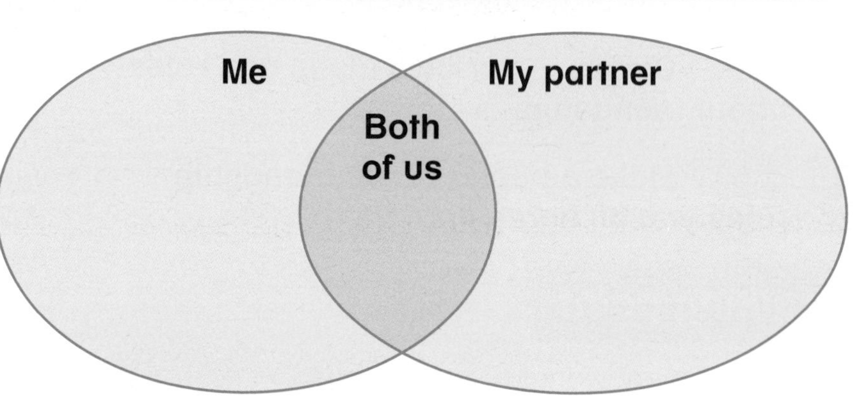

3 **Copy the tally chart and complete it with the five things from your Venn diagram.**

Me	Tally
	I
	I
	I
	I
	I

Key term

tally chart: a way of showing how many times the same thing occurs

4 Look at other Venn diagrams. Complete your tally chart for the class. Add up your tallies.

5 Discuss your results. How similar are the people in your class?

Useful language

I think that we are very/not very/ quite similar because ... of us ...

What do you think? Why?

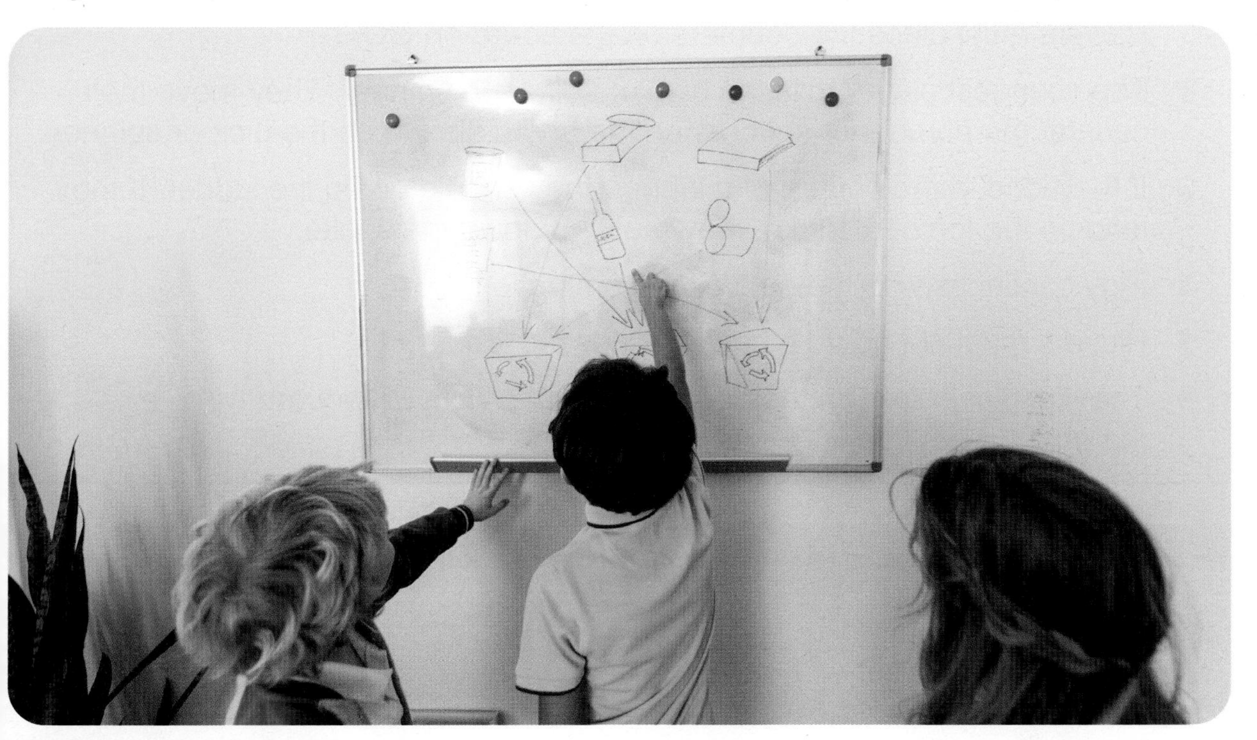

Talking point

Did you enjoy the activities in this lesson? Why, or why not?

How confident are you with showing and reading information in Venn diagrams and tally charts? How confident do you feel about working in a team? Choose green (very confident), amber (getting there) or red (not very confident).

Before you go

How did today's activities help you to answer the question: *How similar are we?*

2.3 Playing the game

✓ **Collaboration**
✓ Communication
✓ Reflection

1 **Read the rules for a game. Look at the pictures and choose the game.**

Game rules

1 Players must place the counters on the board on GO.

2 The youngest player rolls the dice or spins the spinner. They move their counter the number of squares on the board shown on the dice or spinner.

3 If they land at the bottom of a ladder, they should go up the ladder. If they land on the top of a snake, they must go down the snake.

4 Play continues with the next player on the left.

5 Players must not go up a snake or down a ladder.

6 The first player to land their counter on the WINNER square wins the game.

a

b

c

d

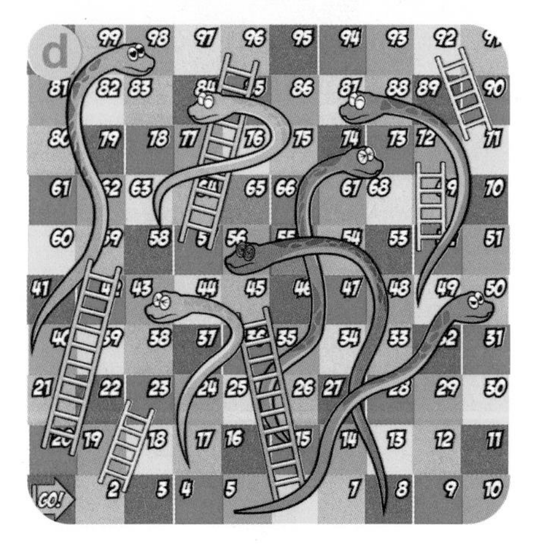

e

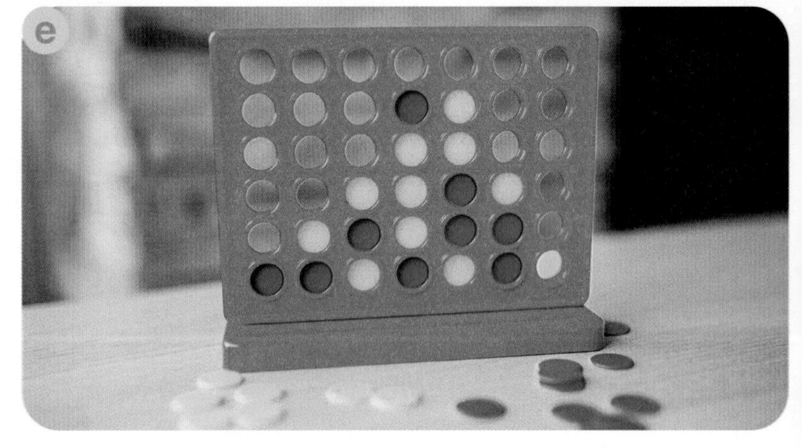

2 Your teacher will give you some more rules to read. Which game are they the rules for? Choose the four rules that best explain the game.

3 Read the 'Group work' checklist. Think of a game you all know well. Write the rules for the game.

Checklist

Group work

- ✓ Take turns to speak.
- ✓ Add a new idea to the group when it is your turn to speak.
- ✓ Listen to other people's ideas.
- ✓ Respond politely and only respond if you can offer a way to improve the suggestion.
- ✓ Check that everyone knows what to write.
- ✓ Help others with spelling or ask for help if you need it.

Useful language

Discussion:

That's a good idea!

We can make it better if we add/take away/include …

What if we say …? Shall we say …?

We need to say that …

Rules:

Players must/must not/have to/should …

If a player (lands on) …, then they …

4 Work in a different group. Read the rules of your game to your new group. Complete the chart on the worksheet.

5 Compare your answers. Vote for the best rules.

Talking point

Use the 'Group work' checklist to answer the questions:

- Did you contribute ideas to your group today?
- Did you help to improve the rules your group wrote? Why or why not?

Before you go

What happens when we do not follow the rules of a game?

2.4 How many rules does our school have?

✓ Research
✓ Analysis

1 What topic is Kai talking about today?

In my classroom we have a 'Golden rules' poster. Do you have one in your classroom?

2 Read the poster. Which rules are the same in your classroom?

3 What other classroom rules do you have? How do you know what the rules are?

4 What do these signs mean? Where might you find them around the school?

5 Let's research! How many rules does your school have? Walk around the school. Take photographs or draw pictures of rules you find. Make notes.

Talking point

How many different signs did you find around the school? Where were most of the signs? How did this investigation help you to answer the question: *How many rules does our school have?*

Do you ever forget the rules or forget to follow them? Why might this happen?

What happens to others if one person forgets the rules?

Before you go

What rule would you add to or take away from your school rules? Why? Write your answers on the worksheet.

2.5 I have some questions

✓ Research

1 **Are there any rules for when you arrive and leave school? What are they?**

2 **Read Kai's messages to Nimalan. What problem is Kai talking about in each one?**

I'm worried about the environment. Lots of students come to school by car and I think this is a big problem. I think we need to travel less by car. I want to find out if other people think it's a problem too and what they think we can do about it.

I was late for school yesterday because the school bus was late. This also happened three times last week. I want to find out if other people are having problems with the buses too and what they think we can do to improve the bus services.

My friend was knocked off his bike outside school yesterday. I think we need to improve safety on the road. I want to find out if other people think it's a problem too and what they think we can do to improve safety outside the school.

3 **Read Nimalan's message to Kai. What does he suggest?**

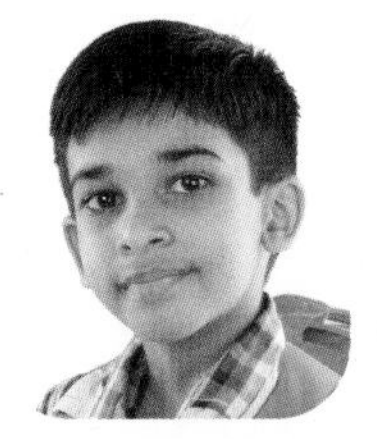

You should make a questionnaire. Then you can ask lots of people.

Key term

questionnaire: a set of questions created to find out what people think about a topic

4 **Kai has written a questionnaire. Match the questionnaire to one of the issues in Activity 2.**

1. How do you or your children travel to school?
2. Do you or your child feel safe outside the school?
3. If you or your child does not travel to school by bike, what is the main reason?
4. How do you think we could make it safer for children to travel to school by bike?

5 Kai has written option answers for three of his questions. Match the options A, B and C below to questions 1–4 in the questionnaire.

A You/they don't have a bike.
You/they can't cycle.
You/they don't think it's safe.

B Yes
No

C By car
By bike
By bus
On foot
Other

Key terms

open question: a question where the person asked can give any answer they want

closed question: a question where the person asked chooses one of several given answers

6 Read the messages. Answer the questions.

a For which type of question can you present the answers in a tally chart or pictogram?

b For which type of question will people be able to give you their own ideas?

Great questions, Kai! Why doesn't question 4 have any options?

Because question 4 is an open question.

7 Make a tally chart for question 2 of the questionnaire. Make a pictogram for question 3.

Subject	Tally	Frequency
Maths	卌 卌 I	11
Reading	卌 II	7
Science	卌	5
Art	卌 卌	10
Music	卌 I	6

Football team	Goals
Mars	●●●●
Jupiter	●●●●●●
Saturn	●●●●●●●●◖
Pluto	●◖
Mercury	●●●●●
Venus	●●●●●●●◖

● = 2 goals

Talking point

Did you learn anything new today? What was it?

Before you go

How do questionnaires help us to research an issue? What types of question can we ask in a questionnaire? What answer would you give to Kai's question 4?

2.6 Can I ask you some questions?

✓ Research
✓ Collaboration
✓ Reflection

1 **Read the rules for the game 'Question chain'. Your teacher will give you some mixed-up questions and answers. Play the game.**

'Question chain' rules

- Pick one question and one answer each.
- The person who most recently had a birthday reads out their question.
- The person with the right answer reads out the answer.
- That person then reads out their question.
- Continue playing until all the answers to the questions have been read out.

2 **Talk about the 'Question Chain' game.**

a What do you think the person who wrote these questions is trying to find out?

b Which questions are or could be closed questions? Choose two and write the option answers for them.

c Choose the five best questions for a questionnaire about food at school.

3 **Read Kai's text message. Match the questions to Kai's messages in Activity 2 of Lesson 5, on page 26.**

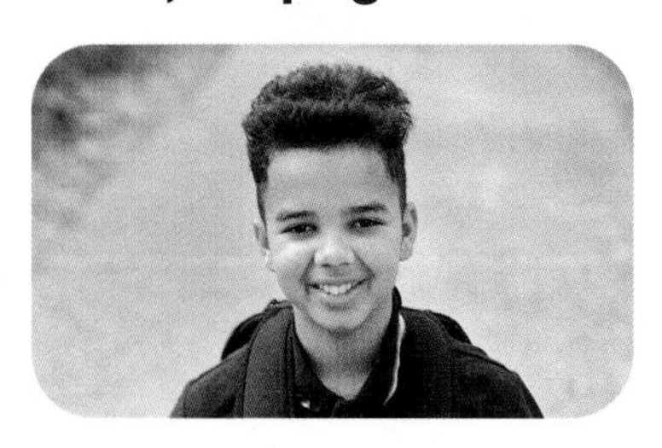

My questions are:

1 Do we need to improve safety outside the school for cyclists? How can we do this?

2 Should we be worried about the environment? What changes can we make to how we travel to school to improve it?

3 How reliable is the school bus service? What would make it better?

4 Play the Running Time! game. Find the questions. Tell your group. Discuss and write the answers.

5 Read the message from Nimalan. Help Kai order the phrases below to make an introduction.

Kai, remember that you need to write an introduction for your questionnaire.

1 Excuse me. My name is …
__ Do you have time to talk to me?
__ I want to find out …
__ Thank you for your time.
__ I'm doing a questionnaire about …
__ There are … questions I'd like to ask you.

6 Write an introduction for one of Kai's other questions.

7 Share your introduction with another group. Rate how well you think you did: bronze, silver or gold.

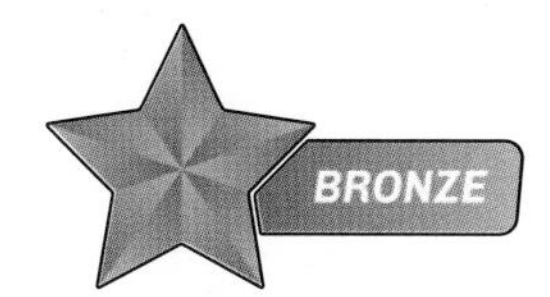

Talking point

Did you work well in a group today? Did you contribute ideas and help to improve your group's answers? Why or why not?

Can you write a questionnaire introduction? Can you write questionnaire questions?

Before you go

Why do we ask questions?

Unit 2 Final task: Create a school rules questionnaire

✓ **Research**
✓ Collaboration
✓ Reflection

Read the final task and discuss the question.

Work in a team of five or six. Think about **rules around your school**. **How successful are they** to help everyone learn, work and play together? **Create a questionnaire** to find out what people think about your school rules and if they can be improved. **Ask people** around the school your questionnaire questions. **Record** some of your findings.

1 What can you do to succeed in this task? Use the words in bold, above, to help you.

2 Choose an area in your school.

a Answer these questions.

1 What do people do in this area?

2 What rules are there in this area?

3 Are there any problems that happen in this area?

4 Why do you think these problems might happen?

b What questions will help you to investigate what people think about each area below, if it needs to be improved and how?

3 Create a questionnaire.

Tips

- Use previous lessons in this unit about school rules to help you with ideas.
- Use the task box at the top of the previous page to help you to do well.
- Use correct question words.
- Think about if a question should be open or closed.
- Check your grammar and spelling before you ask people your questionnaire questions.
- Keep your introduction short.
- Be polite.
- Be a good team member.
- Ask your teacher if you have questions.

4 Write your introduction and practise saying it.

5 Decide …

- Who will you ask?
- When and where will you ask them?
- How many people will you ask?

Tell your teacher.

6 Do your questionnaire.

7 Put your results together. Choose two questions and show the responses in a tally chart or pictogram.

8 Share your findings with the class.

Reflection: How successful was our school rules questionnaire?

a Complete the final task checklist. Use the worksheet, and answer the questions.

Final task checklist			
Our questionnaire helped us to find out how we could improve the school.	☺	😐	☹
Our questionnaire had open and closed questions. They were easy for people to answer.	☺	😐	☹
We asked enough people.	☺	😐	☹
We showed some of our findings in a way that is clear and easy to understand.	☺	😐	☹

b Share your checklist with your team. Do you all agree?

c Take turns to say what you did to help the team. Do you all agree?

Before you go

Discuss these questions with your talking partner.

What did you find out from your questionnaire?
What did you enjoy most about this task?
What did you find most difficult about this task?
Did you need any help during the task? If yes, who did you ask?

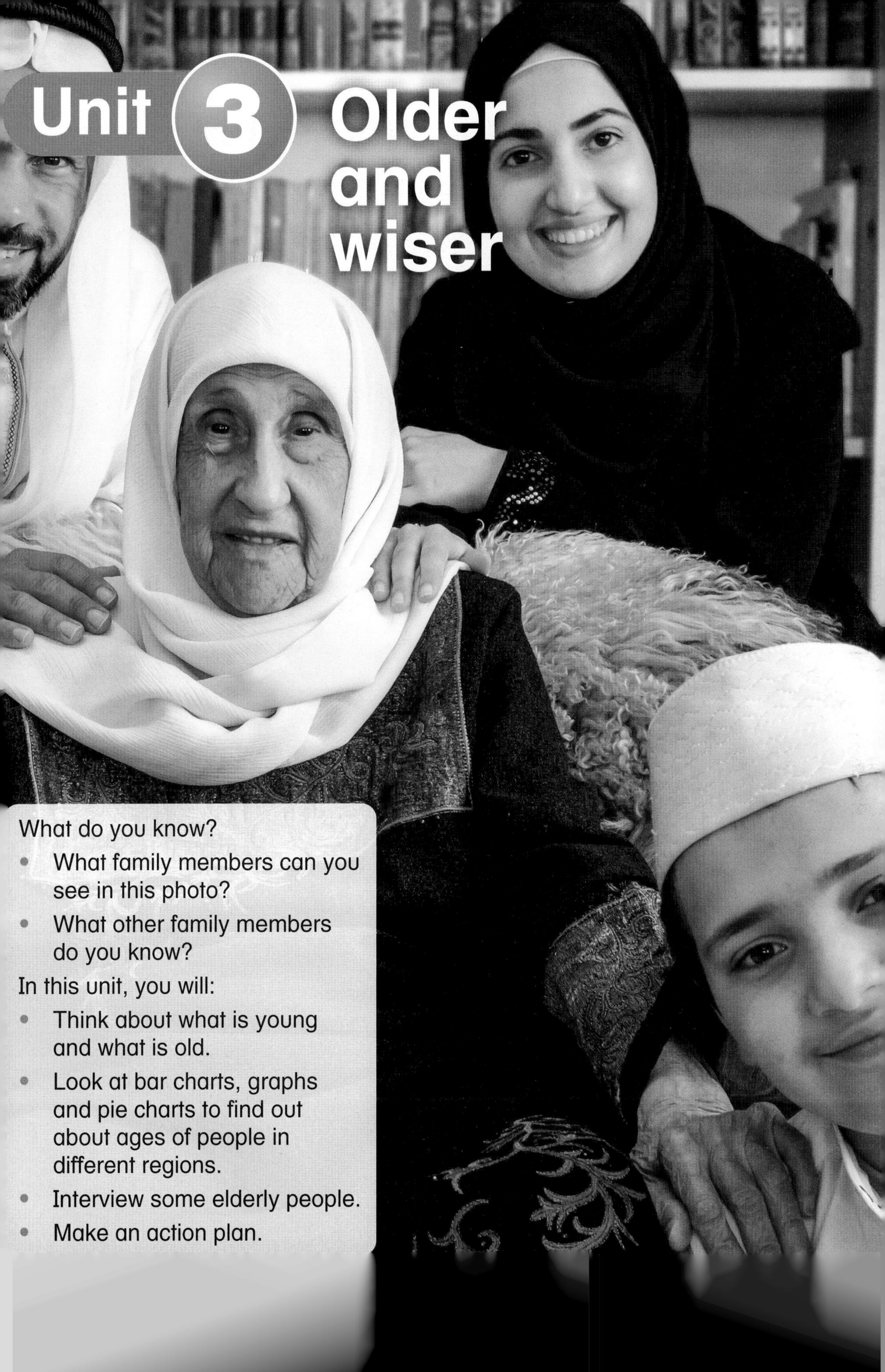

Unit 3 Older and wiser

What do you know?

- What family members can you see in this photo?
- What other family members do you know?

In this unit, you will:

- Think about what is young and what is old.
- Look at bar charts, graphs and pie charts to find out about ages of people in different regions.
- Interview some elderly people.
- Make an action plan.

3.1 What is young? What is old?

✓ **Analysis**
✓ Evaluation

   **Sort the pictures into young and old.**

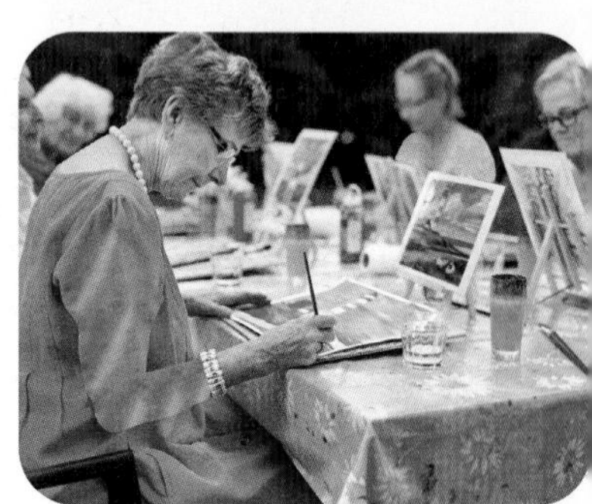

Useful language

I think this person is … because he/she is/has …
I agree/don't agree because …

Hi, I'm Genji. Did your group agree? Do you have different opinions?

2 Look at the human timeline. Choose the best word from the box to describe each stage in the timeline.

adult baby child older person teenager

3 Look at the timeline again. Point to where you are on the timeline. Describe other members of your family. Use words from the box.

4 Look at the storybook cover. Describe the people. Use words from the box in Activity 2.

5 Listen to the story. Put the pictures in the right order.

6 Write answers to Genji's questions on the worksheet.

What does Nan do in the story?

Do you think the author's opinion of older people is positive or negative?

Why do you think this?

Which older people help you?

7 Genji's friends are talking about their older relatives. Who has a positive opinion of being older and who has a negative opinion?

My great-grandmother is quite ill. She can't walk very well. It's not fun being old.
Li Ann

My grandfather cycles in races. He is teaching me to cycle too.
Karam

I love to hug my great-grandmother when she tells me bedtime stories.
Amali

My grandfather is a teacher. He helps me with my homework.
Tenaya

I don't like visiting my grandparents because I have to be very quiet when I am with them.
Machie

Talking point

Did you enjoy the activities in this lesson? How did they help you to answer the questions: *What is young? What is old?*

Before you go

Give one reason why people have different perspectives on issues.

3.2 How many older people are there in Australia?

✓ Analysis
✓ Research

1 Read the infographic. What does it say about how long people are living?

Did you know that all over the world people are living to an older age?

2019

2050 

In 2019, one in every 11 people in the world was 65 or older.

By 2050, around one in six people will be over 65.

Key term

infographic: a text with pictures, numbers and symbols to help us understand information about a topic

2 There are lots of ways to show data. What data does this bar chart tell us?

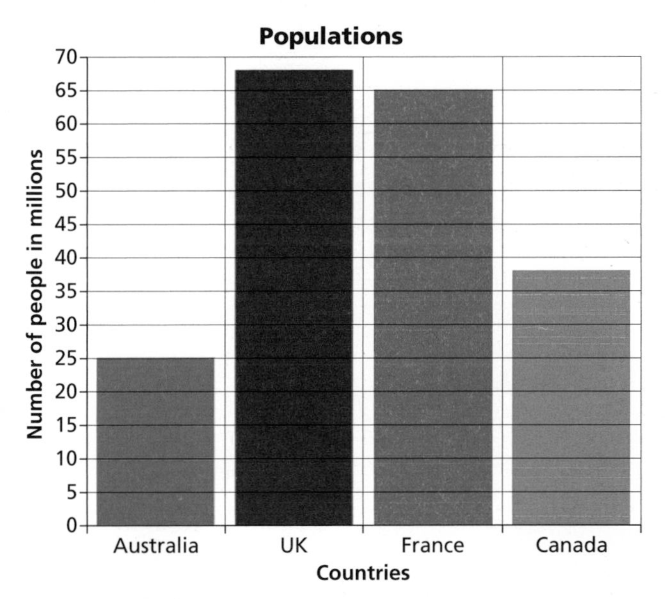

Key terms

data: information or measurements

graph: a picture that shows information about sets of numbers or measurements

pie chart: a circle divided into sections that show how much of the total each thing is

population: the number of people in a country or area

predict: think what will happen in the future

The bar chart tells me how many people live in Australia. But I want to know how many *older* people live in Australia. How can I find out?

3 Now look at another graph. Does it answer Genji's question?

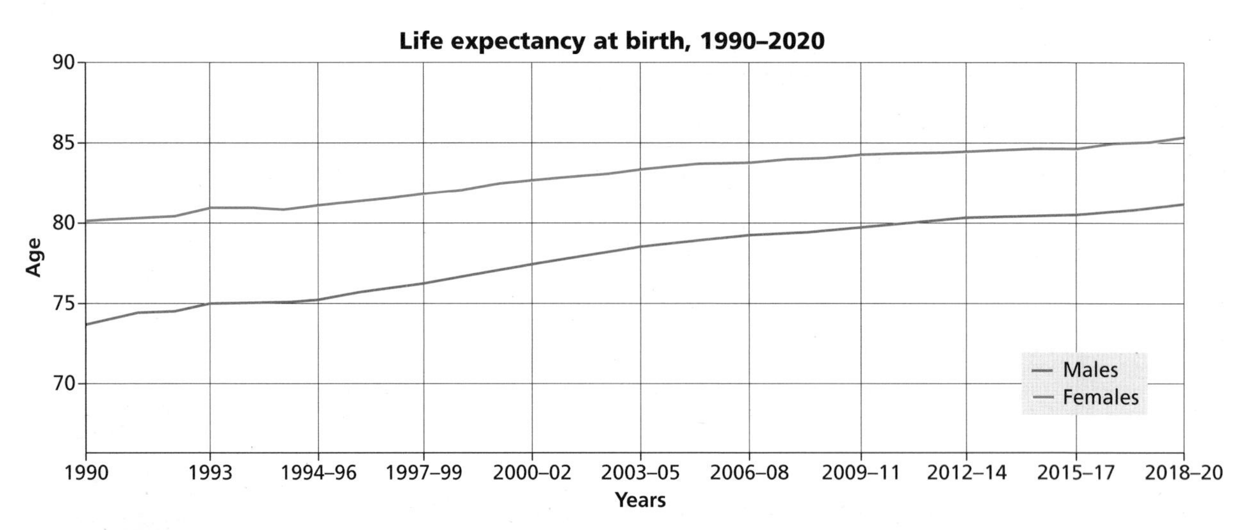

This graph tells me how long people usually lived in different years in Australia. Because the line on the graph goes up as it moves from left to right, I can see that Australians are living longer. So Australia has an ageing population.

4 Does this pie chart answer Genji's question?

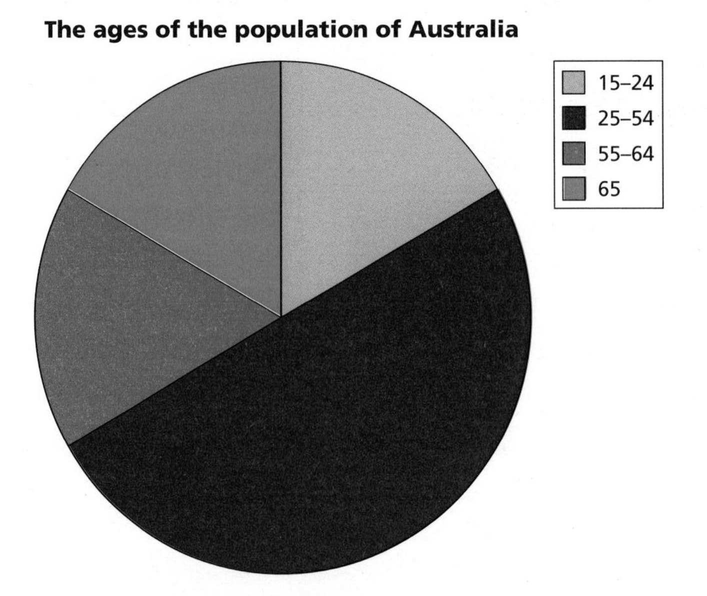

I think this pie chart shows me what age most of the people in Australia are. Do you agree?

5 Now look at another chart. Does this chart help us to answer Genji's question?

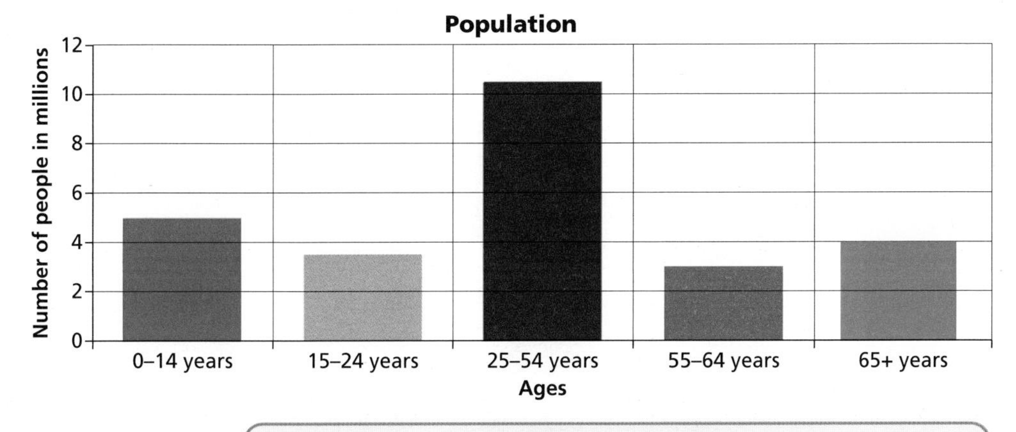

6 Do a graph hunt! Read the sentences. Which graph tells you the information? Some sentences have two sources.

1. Australians are living for longer now than they used to.
2. The population of France is greater than the population of Canada.
3. Most Australians are between 25 and 54.
4. There are 10.5 million Australians between the ages of 25 and 54.
5. There are about the same number of Australians aged between 15 and 24 as there are between 55 and 64.
6. In 1990, most Australian women lived to about 80 years old.

Talking point

How confident do you feel about finding information in graphs and charts? Choose green (very confident), amber (getting there) or red (not very confident).

Before you go

What do you know about the Australian population?

3.3 What do older people do?

✓ **Research**
✓ Collaboration

1 **Look at the pictures. Talk about some of the things older people do and don't do.**

Useful language

Elderly people sometimes/never … do/don't …
go to school/university, do sport/yoga/painting …

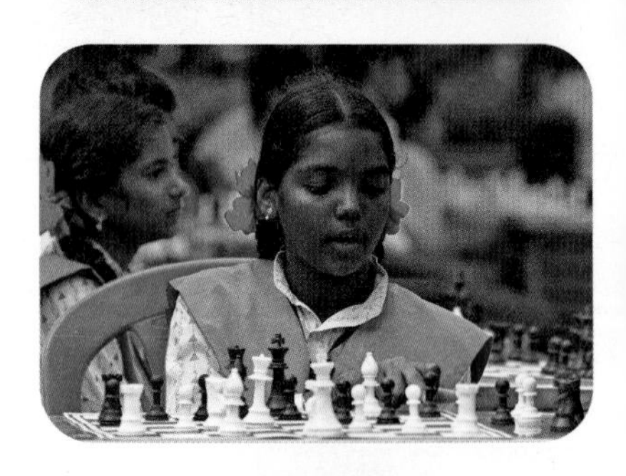

2 **Read and answer Genji's question.**

3 Help Genji find out more about what older people do. Write five questionnaire questions.

My friend says a good question is: *What do you like to do?* I don't think it is a good question. What do you think?

4 Compare your answers. Vote for the best questions.

5 Is it important to have activities and roles for older people in our society? Think of another question you could ask to find out what older people would like to be able to do.

Talking point

How well did you work together today?
Did you remember how to write questionnaire questions?
Can you explain open and closed questions to your partner?
Use an example.

Before you go

Now you have your questionnaire questions, who will you get to answer them?

3.4 What's important to older people?

✓ **Research**
✓ Evaluation

1 Look at the ideas map on the worksheet. What is it about?

2 Write down one more way of recording an interview to add to the ideas map.

3 Add the + and – points to your ideas map. Then add some + or – sentences for your extra way of recording information.

+ You can hear the exact words a person said.

+ You can play the recording as many times as you need to.

+ You can see and hear the speaker.

+ You can choose only the most important information to record.

– You have to be able to write quickly and clearly.

– You can't record everything you hear.

– You have to make notes from the recording later.

– You may miss some important information.

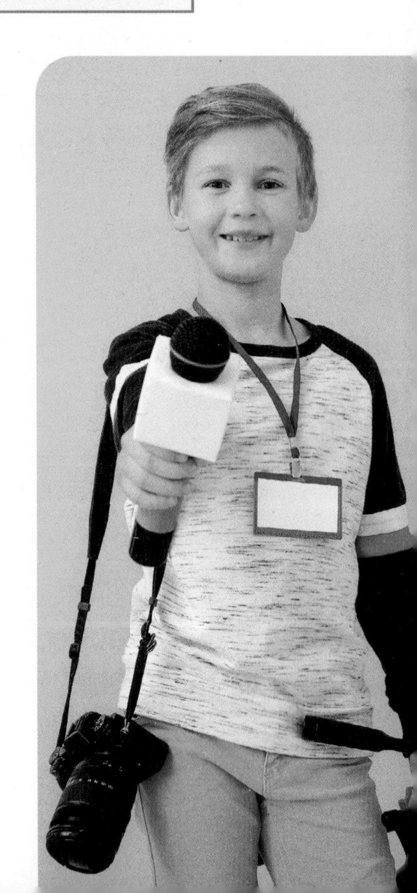

4 Look at the ideas map again. How will you record your interviews?

5 Use your questionnaire to interview some older people.

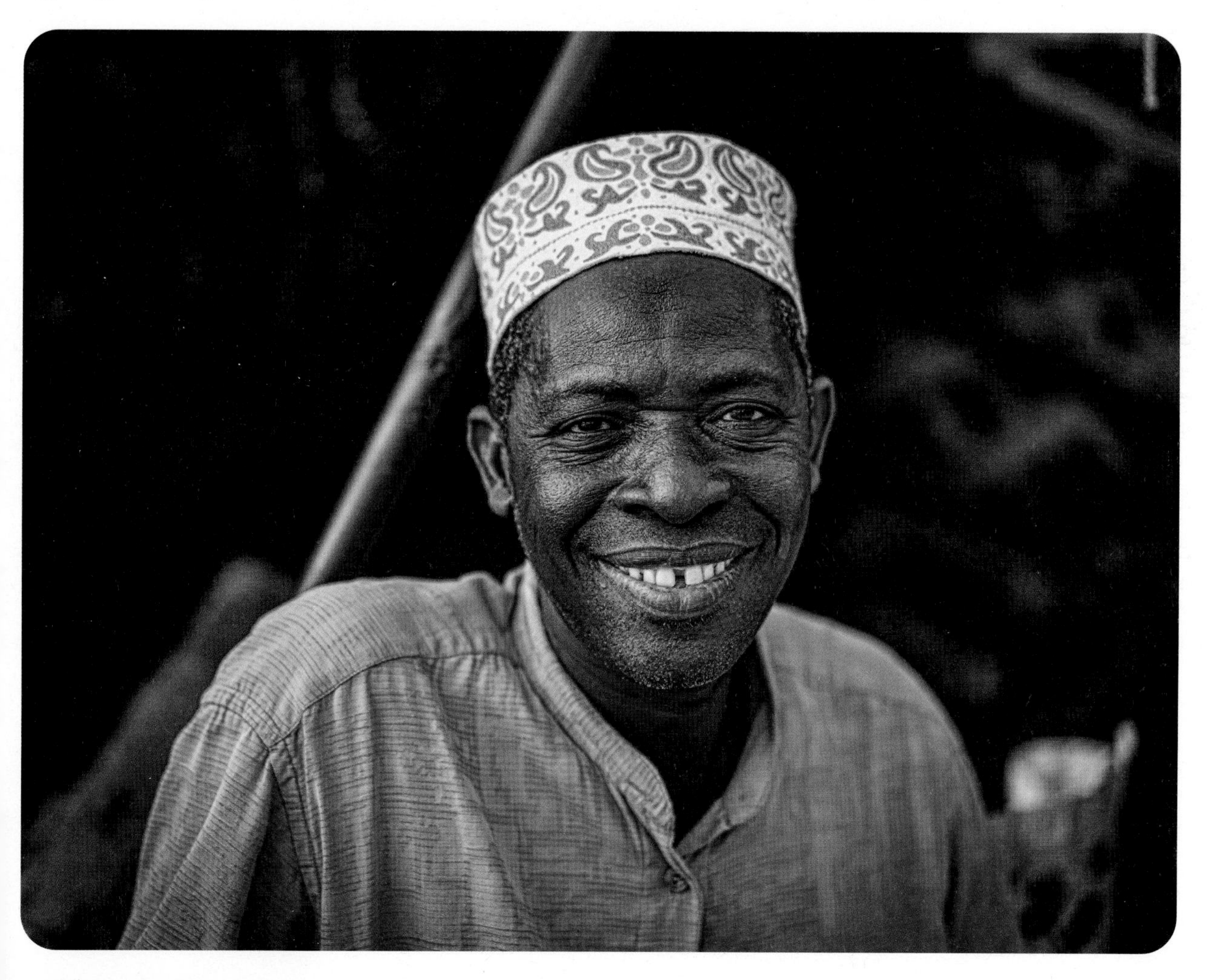

Talking point

Did you enjoy today's interview? Did you learn anything new? Were you surprised by anything? Complete the exit ticket on the worksheet.

Before you go

Name something that the people you interviewed think is important.

3.5 What do we know and think about older people?

✓ Research
✓ Analysis

1 **Read the message from Genji. Can you answer her question? Use the flow chart to help you decide.**

The interviews were great! What do we do next?

Set a big question. → Write questions to help find out information. → Do an investigation. → Select and record the information that helps us to answer our big question.

2 **Can you remember some different ways to record information? What type of charts or graphs can you use? Choose one type and record the information for your question.**

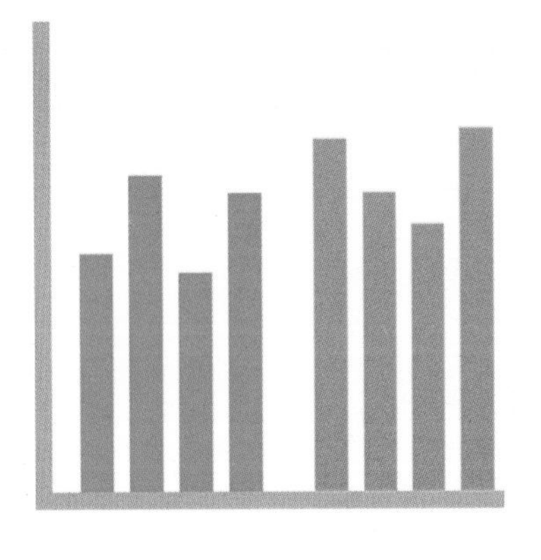

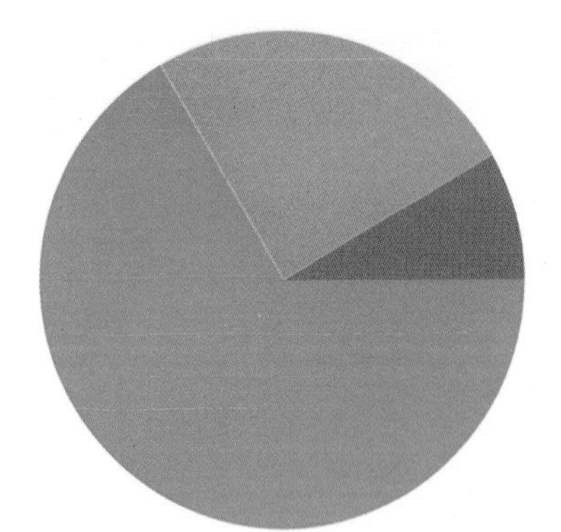

3 What have you found out? What conclusions can you make?

Key term

conclusion: a statement that is made after looking carefully at results

4 How did this research help you to answer the questions: ***What do older people do?*** **and** ***What's important to older people?***

5 Read and answer Genji's question.

How do you think the people you interviewed feel about being older?

6 Make a list of activities that older people like to do. Compare your list with a partner. Do these activities help people to stay fit and well?

Older people like to:

- *go to yoga classes*

Talking point

Tell a partner something you have learned about older people.

Before you go

Write down one thing that you have learned today that you think is interesting or useful.

3.6 How can we make an age-friendly community?

✓ **Communication**
✓ Research
✓ Collaboration

1 **Read the text quickly. What is WHO?**

The letters WHO stand for the **W**orld **H**ealth **O**rganization. WHO helps people all over the world to be healthy and well in their bodies and minds.

2 **Read the text. What should all cities and communities try to do?**

The United Nations (UN) says that between 2019 and 2050 the number of older people in the world may double. That means there will be nearly twice as many older people in 2050 than there are now.

Because of this, the WHO has set up a network that connects cities and communities around the world. It aims to make them into great places for older people.

3 **Can you find your community on the map? Is your community part of the WHO Global network for age-friendly communities?**

4 Play 'Running Time!' Find four topics that the WHO thinks are important for age-friendly communities.

5 Match each statement below to one of the four topics.

Lots of flowers, trees and lakes around the town or city

Cheap, frequent and easy to use; places to sit while you wait

Close to shops so you can walk there; in safe neighbourhoods

Doctor's surgeries and pharmacies that are easy to get to

6 Design an information poster for one of the topics.

Top tips

- Use images: do drawings, cut out pictures from magazines, take photos or print out pictures from the internet.
- Use different colours.
- Write neatly and check your spelling.
- Use the whole sheet of paper.

7 Present your poster to another group. Give feedback on their poster.

Talking point

Did you work well in a group today? Did you contribute ideas and help to improve your group's poster?

Before you go

How age-friendly do you think our community is?

Unit 3 Final task: Plan an age-friendly community

✓ **Analysis**
✓ Collaboration
✓ Reflection

Read the final task and discuss the question.

Work in a team of five or six. **Analyse information** to find out if your community has an ageing population. Think about what this means for your community. Does your community need to be age friendly? **Do some research** to see how age friendly your community is. Work in a group to **make a plan** for you and your friends to do to help **make your community more age friendly.**

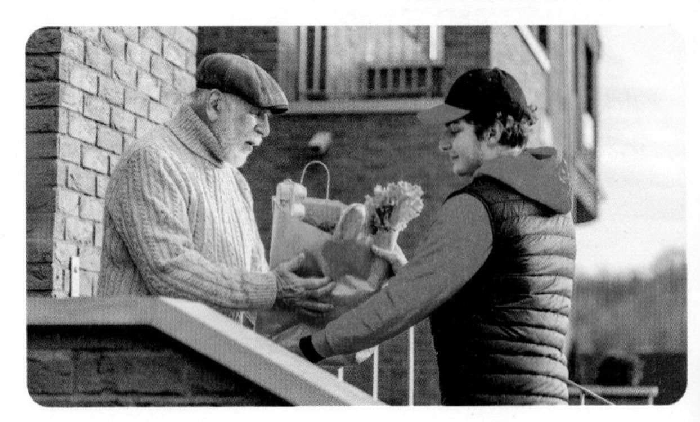

1 What can you do to succeed in this task? Use the words in bold, in the box above the photos, to help you.

Tips

- Use previous lessons in this unit to help you to understand the information.
- Use the words in bold to help you do the task well.
- Ask your teacher if you have questions.

2 Look at the information your teacher gives you and answer the questions.

1 How many people over 65 live in your community?

2 What age are most of the people in your community?

3 Is this the same as or different from ten years ago?

4 Does your community need to be age friendly? Why or why not?

3 Let's find out! How age friendly is your community? Complete the ideas map on the worksheet.

4 Now write your plan. Think! How will your plan make a positive difference to the issue?

Our action is to …
This relates to the issue of …
We will do our action (where) …
We will do our action (when) …
To do our action, we will need …

Reflection: How successful was our age-friendly community plan?

a Complete the final task checklist. Use the worksheet.

Final task checklist			
We understood the information about population ages in our region and this helped us to think of ways to improve our community.	☺	😐	☹
Our action plan shows at least one useful thing we can do to help our community to be age friendly.	☺	😐	☹
Everyone in our group made suggestions.	☺	😐	☹

b Share your checklist with your team. Do you all agree?

c Take turns to say what you did to help the team. Do you all agree?

Before you go

Discuss these questions with your talking partner.

What did you find out from the information your teacher gave you?
What did you enjoy most about this task?
What did you find most difficult about this task?
Did you need any help during the task? If yes, who did you ask?
What do you think you have learned in this unit?

Unit 4 A fair life!

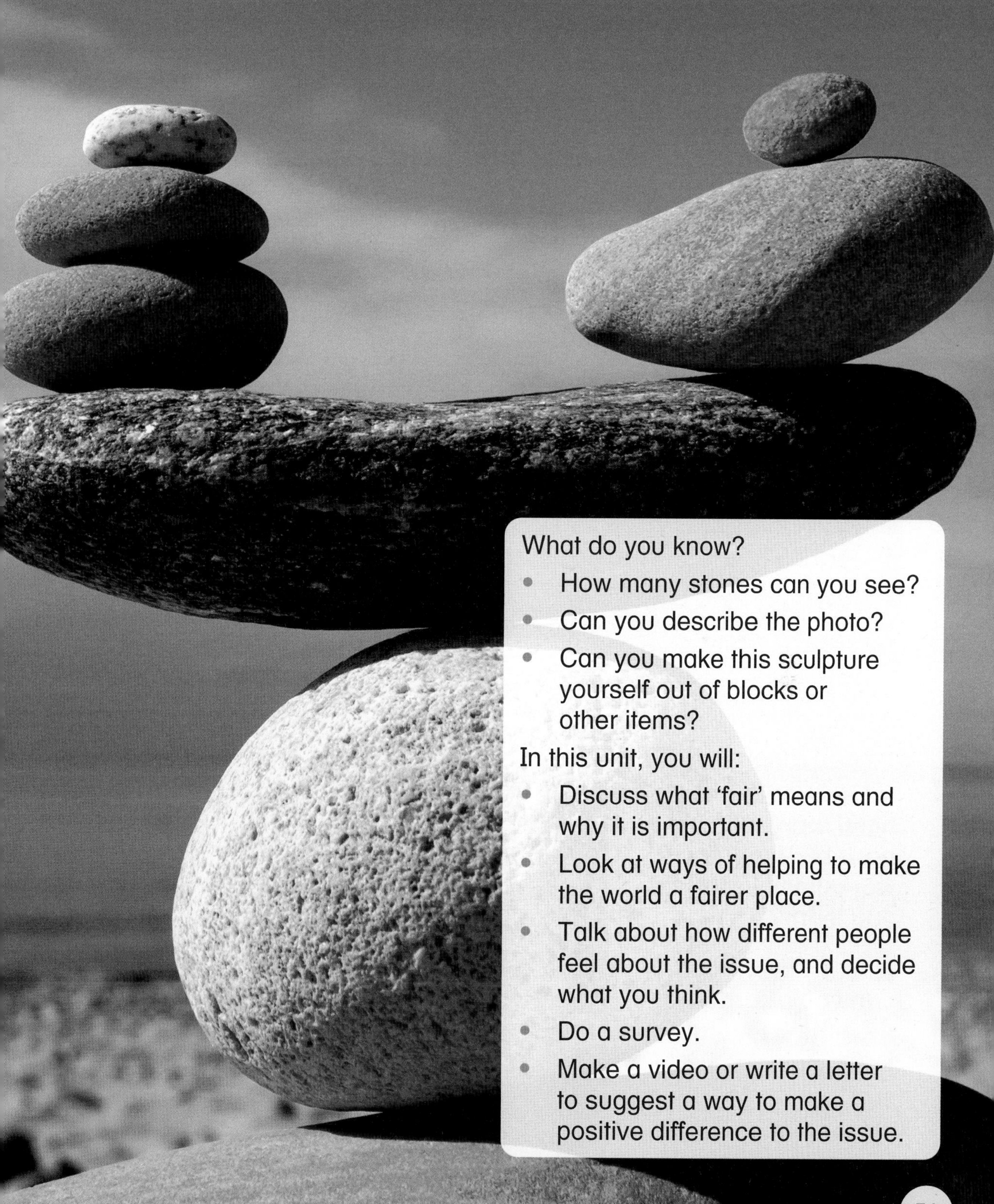

What do you know?

- How many stones can you see?
- Can you describe the photo?
- Can you make this sculpture yourself out of blocks or other items?

In this unit, you will:

- Discuss what 'fair' means and why it is important.
- Look at ways of helping to make the world a fairer place.
- Talk about how different people feel about the issue, and decide what you think.
- Do a survey.
- Make a video or write a letter to suggest a way to make a positive difference to the issue.

4.1 What does 'fair' mean?

✓ **Evaluation**
✓ Analysis
✓ Reflection

1 Read Kai's message to Jomo. Answer his questions.

Hi Jomo. I'm doing a project about rich and poor. Can you help me? What does 'fair' mean? Is it important?

2 Read Jomo's reply. What does he suggest Kai does?

Hi Kai. I know a story you can read with a friend to find out what 'fair' means. Then you can tell me if you think it's important.

3 Read Jomo's hotel story with a partner. Use the worksheet. What did you learn?

4 Which room can you afford in the hotel? Is it fair?

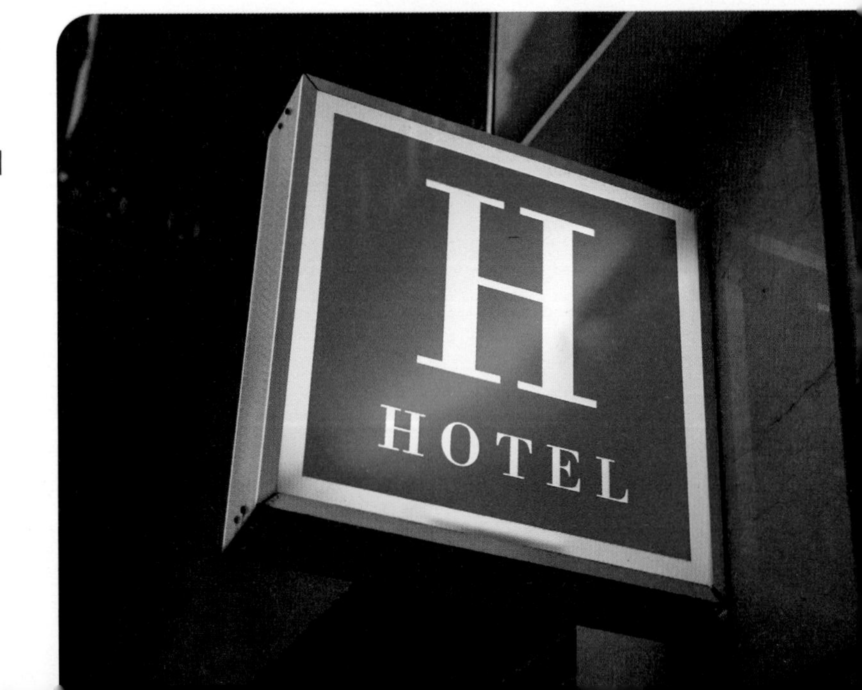

5 Read Kai's message. Use the pictures to help you write a reply.

What can I do to help people who don't have as much as me?

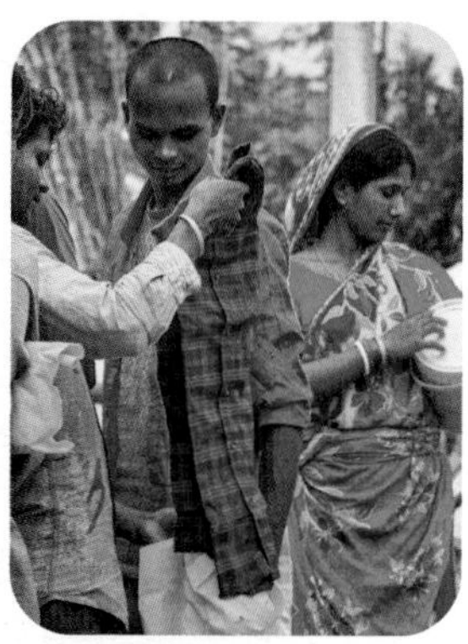

6 Read about charity. What three things do people give?

Charity is about helping other people. It can be giving money, things or time to people who need it.

Useful language

We can help other people by donating/helping/giving …

People donate/help/give … to people who don't have enough.

7 Read the messages from Jomo and Nimalan. Do they have the same opinions about charity?

Charity is important because so many people are in need. It's the best way to help people.

Charity does help people because they get the things they need quickly, but it doesn't make life fair. I think it's better to help people to make more money so they can always buy the things they need.

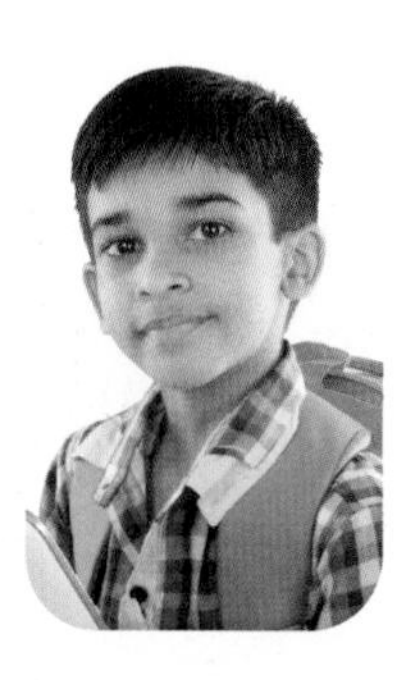

Talking point

Did you enjoy the activities in this lesson? Tell your partner the activity you enjoyed most and why. What did you learn doing this activity?

Before you go

What do you think 'fair' means? Do you agree more with Jomo or with Nimalan?

4.2 What do you need?

✓ **Analysis**
✓ Evaluation
✓ Research

1 **What could you do with these things?**

2 **Match the photos in Activity 1 with where they come from. Use the words.**

honey bees   alpaca   wheat plant   coffee beans

3 **If you did not have much money, would you rather have the first four things or the second four things? Why? Use the words in the box.**

make   sell

4 Read Rosa's story. Match it to an item in Activity 2.

Two years ago my family was very poor and life was very hard for us.

A charity gave us clothes. They were nice and warm, but we were still hungry.

Then, we were given three alpacas. My father and mother were taught how to look after the alpacas properly and how to make wool from the alpacas' fur.

Now, they make beautiful clothes out of the wool and we sell them.

Now my family has more money. We are much happier and I can go to school.

Rosa, aged 7

5 Act out Rosa's story.

6 Copy and complete the chart about Rosa's life.

Two years ago	Now
poor no alpacas	more money

7 Read Jomo and Nimalan's messages from the last lesson. Who do you think Rosa agrees with?

Talking point

Did the text make you change your mind about your answer to the question in Activity 3?

How confident are you in recognising what someone thinks about an issue? Choose green (very confident), amber (getting there) or red (not very confident).

Before you go

Can you name something you need?

4.3 What is fair trade?

✓ **Research**
✓ Reflection

1 Read Kai's message. What is his project about?

My school project is about fair trade. I don't know what it is, and I don't know how to start. Can you help me?

Key term
trade: buying and selling goods

2 Read Jomo's reply. What does he suggest?

You should make a KWL chart. It will help you to see what you already know, what you want to know and what you have learned. K = Know, W = Want to know and L = Learned. KWL.

3 Start a KWL chart about fair trade. Use the worksheet.

4 Kai has written some questions. Which part of his KWL chart should he write them in?

a What is fair trade?
b Why is fair trade important?
c What fair trade foods can we buy?

5 Use the infographic to help Kai answer his questions. Can you answer all three?

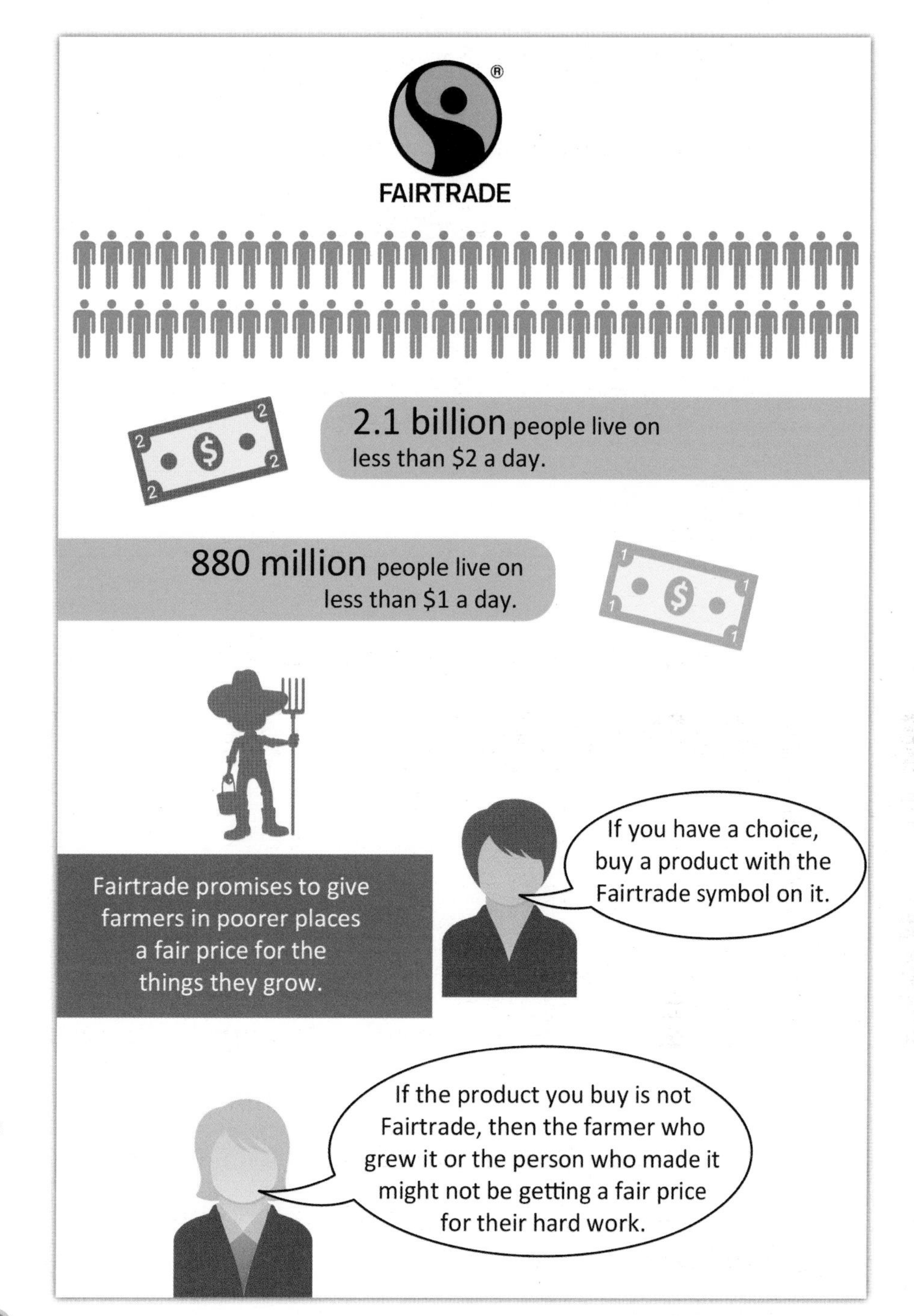

6 Add answers to Kai's questions to your KWL chart.

7 Do the speakers in the infographic have the same or different opinions?

Talking point

How can a KWL chart help us to work on a project? How useful was the infographic? What do you like about the infographic?

Complete the 3-2-1 reflection ticket on the worksheet that your teacher will give you.

Before you go

Where else could we find information about fair trade?

4.4 What fair trade foods can we buy?

✓ **Research**
✓ Reflection

1 **Play 'Draw it!' Your teacher will give you the cards you need to play.**

2 **Add any new information to your KWL chart.**

3 **Play 'Snakes and Flowers'. Use the game board on the next page.**

4 **Add to your KWL chart.**

Talking point

How did these games help you to learn more about fair trade?

Before you go

Are you becoming a fair trade expert? What new information do you know about fair trade?

Key term

expert: a person who knows a lot about a topic

FINISH
34
33
You sell your flowers for a fair price
32
31
Not enough people buy Fairtrade
30
24
The price of fuel for your truck goes up
25
26
27
28
Your village gets a new teacher and the children can go to school
29
23
22
21
20
You move into a new house
19
18
12
You're sick and you can't harvest your flowers
13
14
You start to grow more flowers
15
16
Friends in your cooperative help you to pick your flowers
17
11
10
9
A storm ruins your flowers
8
7
6
START
1
2
You become a Fairtrade farm and part of a cooperative
3
4
5
You learn to cut waste on your farm

4.5 The journey

✓ **Collaboration**
✓ Research

1. **Choose a fair-trade product. Find out where it is grown or made.**

2. **Look at the fact file on the worksheet. What information do you need to find out for your product? Research your product. Then complete the fact file.**

Key term

fact file: a way to record information about a place, a person or a thing

3. **Design a comic that shows your product's fair-trade journey. Use the 'Top tips' to help you.**

Top tips

- Before you start drawing or writing, plan your comic. How many different pictures will you need?
- Decide as a group, who is good at drawing and colouring, who is good at writing?
- Draw squares and rectangles on your paper to show where each picture will go. Where will the words go? Use the whole sheet of paper.
- Draw your pictures. Use different colours.
- Write neatly and check your spelling.
- Stick your pictures and writing onto your paper.

4 **Present your comic to another group. Give the other group feedback on their comic:**

- What was good?
- What could they improve?

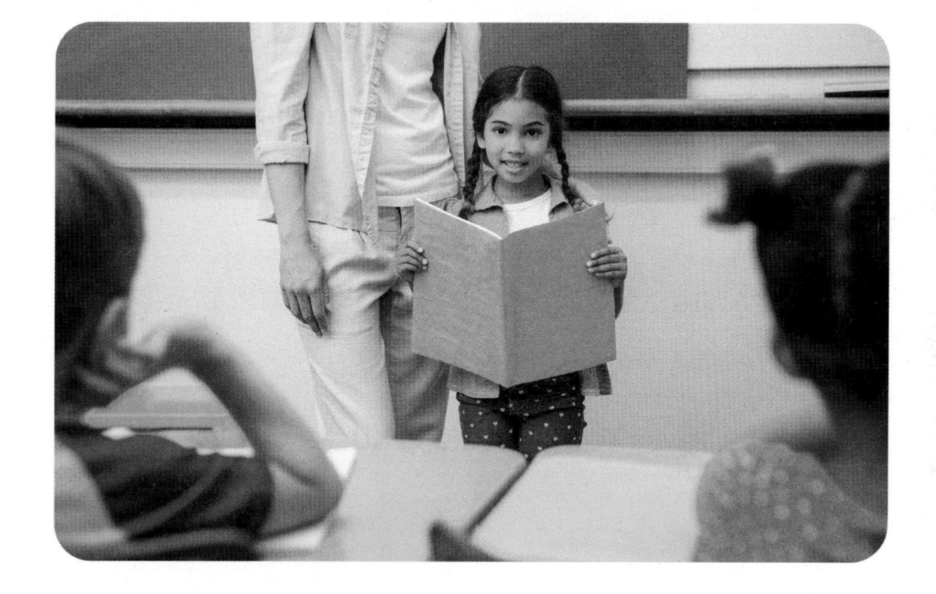

Talking point

Did you enjoy your role in the group? Why or why not? Is there a different role you would like to try next time? Why? Did you contribute ideas and help to improve your group's comic? Why or why not?

Before you go

Do you think it's easy for most fair-trade products to get to shops or onto dinner tables?

4.6 Do you agree about fair trade?

✓ **Evaluation**
✓ Research
✓ Analysis

1 **Read Kai's message. What do you think?**

Wow! I know so much about fair trade now. Does everyone know about it?

2 **Read Jomo's reply. What does he suggest?**

Good question, Kai.
Why don't you ask some people? You can do a survey.

3 **Let's write a survey question! Ask yourself:**

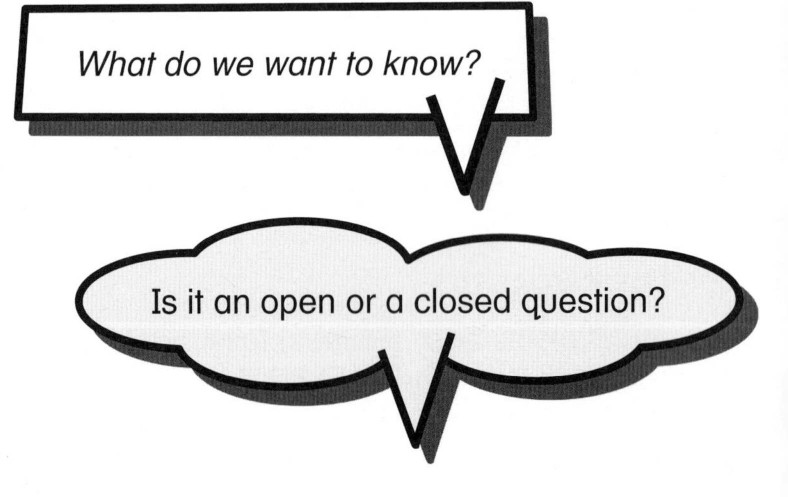

4 Survey some people. Record the results.

5 How can you show the results of your survey?

6 Do a lot of people know about fair trade? Is this good or bad? Why? Discuss your ideas.

7 Read Nimalan's message and answer his questions.

Do you think fair trade changes farmers' lives? Does it make a difference if we do or don't buy fair-trade things when we can?

8 Read these people's opinions of fair trade. Do you agree or disagree with them? Explain why.

It's not fair that I have to pay more for fair-trade things than non-fair-trade things.

Buying fair-trade things is a brilliant way to make the world fairer.

People are only poor because they don't work hard enough.

I know some people are poor, but there's nothing I can do to help.

Useful language

My personal opinion is that …

In my opinion …

I think/believe that …

… because …

Talking point

How many people did you ask in your survey? Were you surprised by the survey results? Why or why not?

Before you go

What is your opinion about fair trade now?

Unit 4 Final task: Create a letter or video about fair trade

✓ **Evaluation**
✓ Collaboration
✓ Analysis
✓ Reflection

Read the final task and discuss the question.

Work in **teams** of five or six. Discuss charity and fair trade as ways of helping others. Write some answers to questions about fair trade and then **give your opinion about other class members' views**. Use your knowledge of fair trade to **write a letter or make a video** to **persuade someone to buy or to sell fair-trade goods**. Give your opinion of fair trade and **explain how the things we do can make a difference to someone else's life**.

1 **What can you do to succeed in this task? Use the words in bold, in the box above, to help you.**

2 **As a group, answer the questions your teacher gives you. Every person in the group must write the answer to at least one question. Use your KWL charts from this unit to help you.**

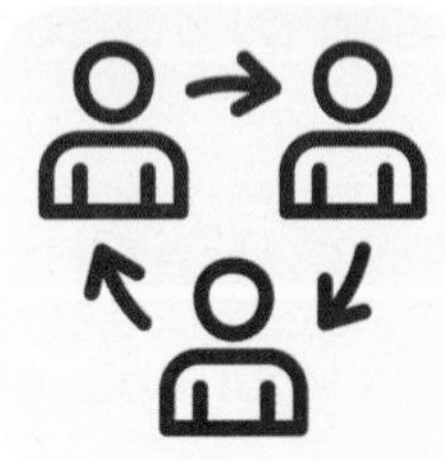

3 Swap papers with another group. Read their answers. Say if you agree or disagree with their ideas. Give reasons why you agree or disagree.

4 Read Jomo's message and answer his question.

Who will you send your letter or show your video to?

5 Write your letter or record your video. Remember: you want to persuade people to make a positive difference to the issue.

The issue we want to talk about is being fair. Being fair is important because …
The world isn't fair because lots of people don't have/can't …
Have you heard about fair trade? Fair trade is …
You can buy/sell … This helps people who … They can …
We agree that fair trade is good because …

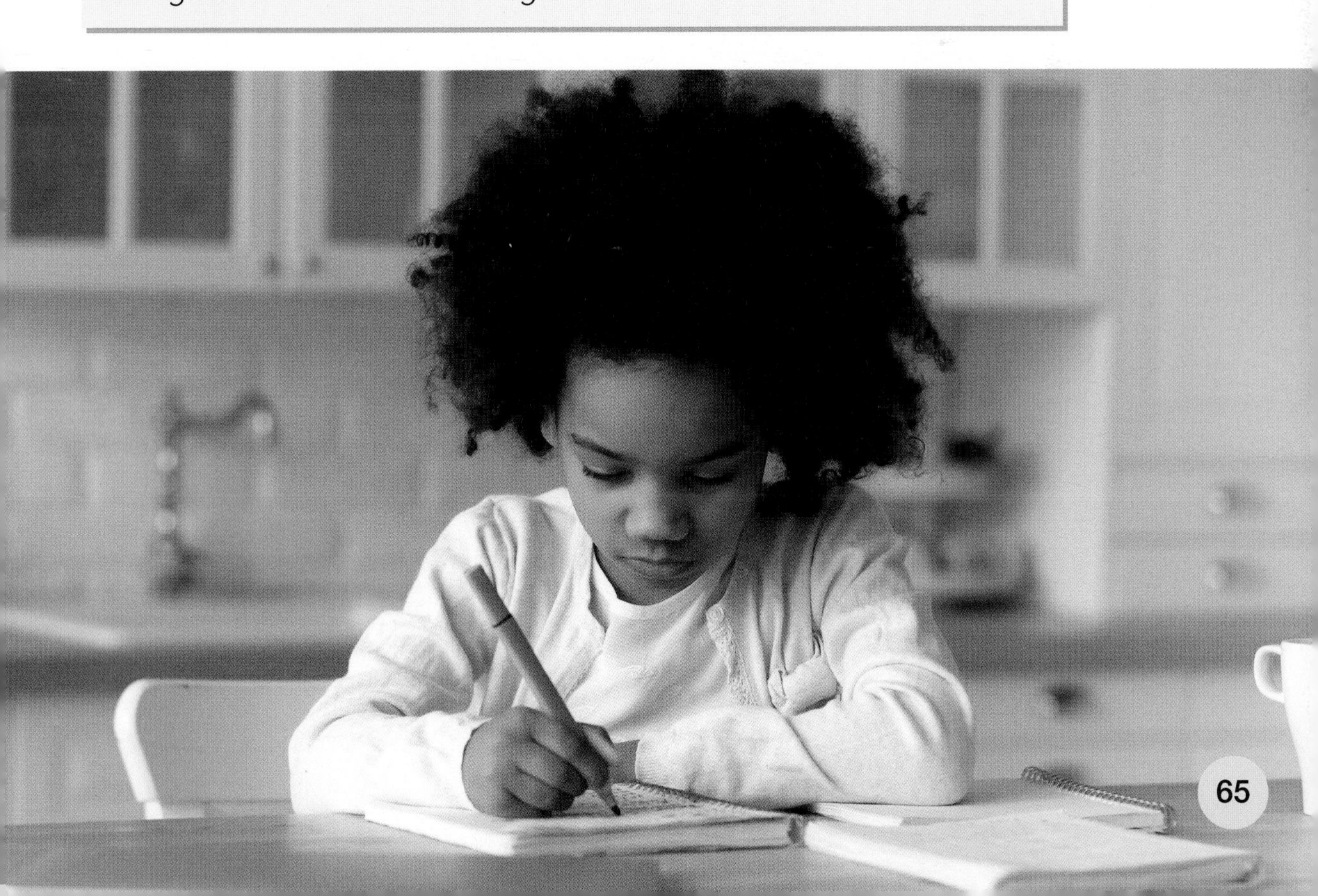

Reflection: How successful was our letter or video?

a Complete the final task checklist. Use the worksheet.

Final task checklist			
Our letter or video helps a person or people to understand what fair trade is.	☺	😐	☹
Our letter or video explains why fair trade is important.	☺	😐	☹
Our letter or video clearly shows our opinions.	☺	😐	☹
Our letter or video suggests what someone can do to make a positive difference.	☺	😐	☹

b Share your checklist with your team. Do you all agree?

c Take turns to say what you did to help the team. Do you all agree?

Before you go

Discuss these questions with your talking partner.

Did you give your opinions on your classmates' opinions?
Did your group produce a letter or a video?
Were you happy with your letter or video? Why, or why not?
What did you enjoy most about this task?
What did you find most difficult about this task?
Did you need any help during the task? If yes, who did you ask?

Unit 5 You are welcome!

What do you know?

- How many different languages can you see?
- What word do they all say?
- How do you say this word in your languages?

In this unit, you will:

- Think about why people move to a new country.
- Think about how a new place might feel different and how the person might feel there.
- Look at ways of helping to make a new person feel welcome where you live.
- Make a video to welcome a new student to your class.

5.1 Where do our families come from?

✓ **Research**
✓ Communication

1 Find out more about your teacher. Ask questions.

2 Do we all come from the same place? Mark where your family is from on the map.

3 Read Anya's message. What does she want to find out?

Lots of my friends' families come from places different to mine. What questions can I ask to find out all about their families?

4 Write some questions for Anya to ask her friends. Everyone in your group should write at least one question.

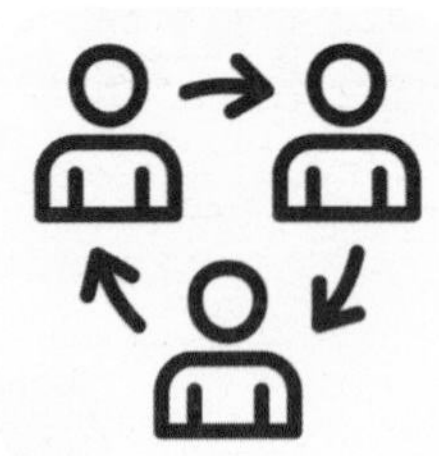

5 Read the message. What is Genji's talking tip?

Hi, Anya. Asking questions is a fun way to learn something new about a person. Just remember to use your inside voices so you can all hear each other.

6 Find out about your partner's family. Record the information on the worksheet.

7 Use the pictures to help you write some speaking top tips. Are these people doing a good job?

8 Present the information you have found out about your partner to another pair.

Key term

present: to show, tell or explain something to others

Useful language

I found out that …

I was surprised to learn that …

Did you know that …?

Talking point

Did you remember the speaking top tips when you were talking with your partner and in groups?

Before you go

Do all our families come from the same place? What do you think we can learn from people who come from another place?

5.2 What is migration?

✓ **Communication**
✓ Research

1 **Read Anya's message. What does she want to find out?**

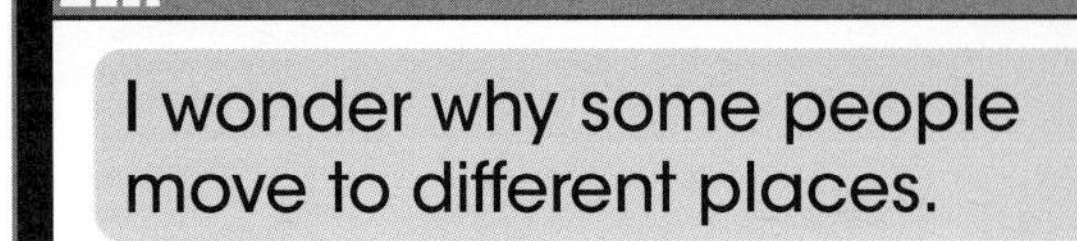

2 **Read Genji's reply. What does she suggest?**

I have some information about animals that move to different places. Maybe that will help you?

3 **Read about an animal journey. Find the places in your text on a map of the world.**

4 **Underline the most important information in your text.**

5 **Share what you know in a new group.**

6 **Answer these questions.**

a What is migration?

b Which animal migrates the furthest?

c Why do animals migrate?

7 **Read Anya's message. Is she right?**

I think migration is when an animal or a person moves to a new place for part of the year and then moves back to their original place.

Talking point

How confident are you at presenting information in small groups? Choose green (very confident), amber (getting there) or red (not very confident).

Before you go

Do you think people move to new places for the same reasons as animals?

5.3 What is different about our countries?

✓ **Communication**
✓ Research

1 **Read the title and look at the pictures. Answer the questions.**

a Which city is this text about?

b Is it a modern city or a traditional city? Why do you think this?

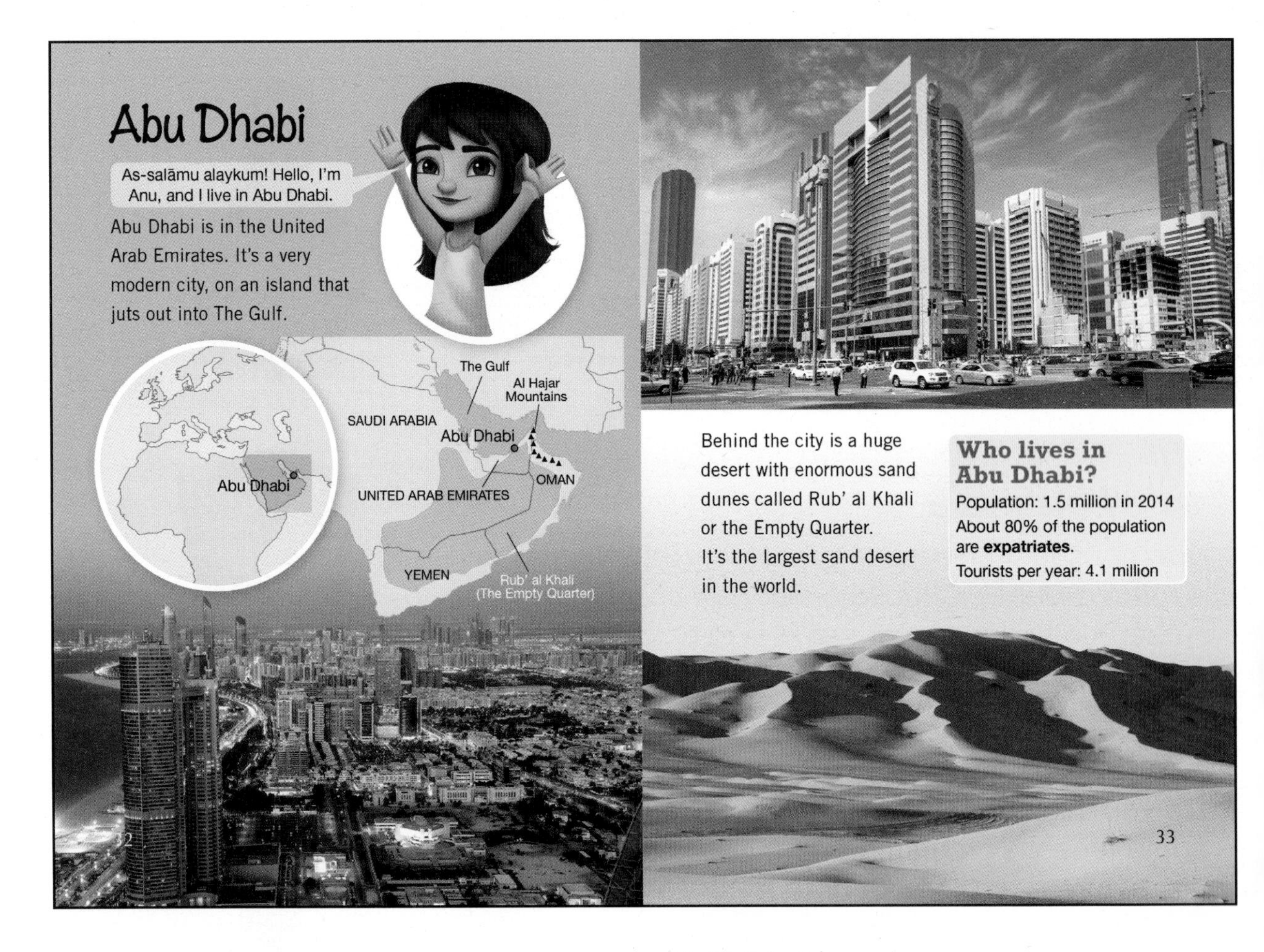

2 **Read the text. How is Abu Dhabi the same as or different from where you live?**

Key term

expatriate: person who lives outside the country where they were born

3 Read what the girl says. Where do you think she lives?

Bonjour! Hi, I'm Manon.

4 Read the text. How is Paris the same as or different from where you live?

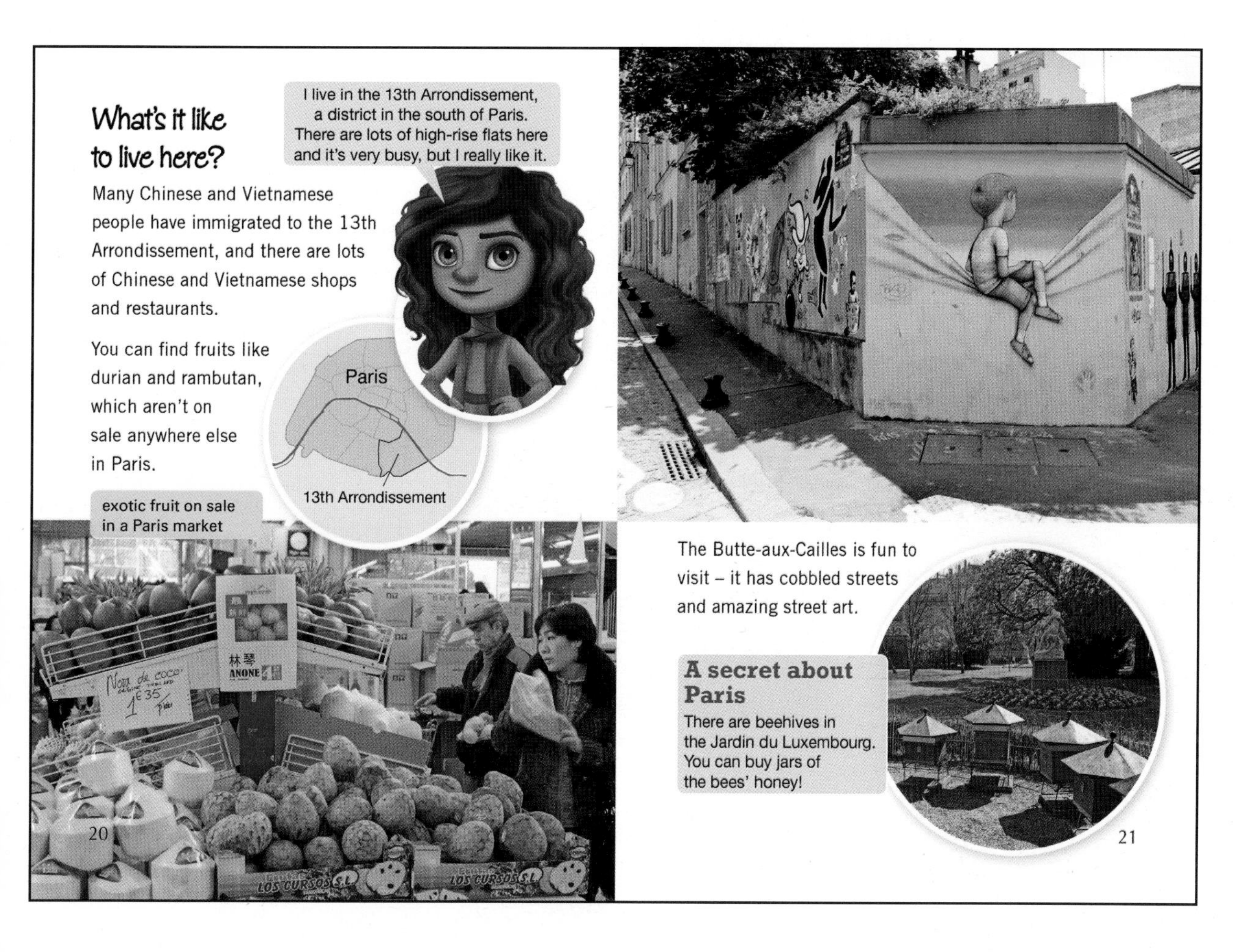

5 Write questions to ask Anu and Manon.

What is it like to live in your city?
What can you ...?
What ...?
Is it ...?
Do you have ...?

6 You are going to read a conversation between Anu and Manon. First, make a conversation checklist.

Conversation checklist

- Sit up straight and face the person you are speaking with.
-
-

7 Work in groups of four. In two pairs, read the conversation on the worksheet. Watch and listen to the other pair. Are they following the points on your checklist? Give each other feedback.

8 Would you like to live in Abu Dhabi or Paris? Why or why not?

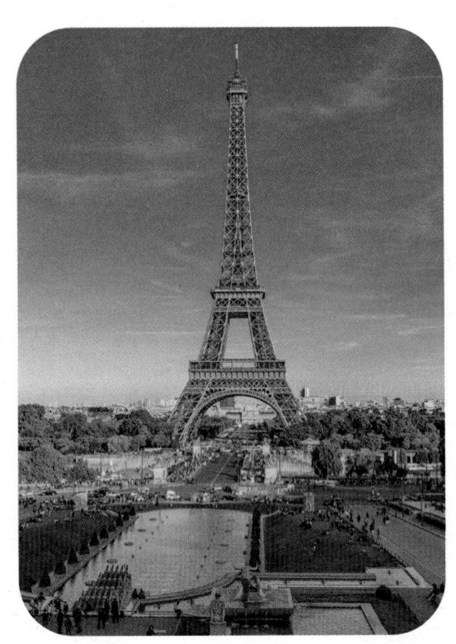

Talking point

How good were you and your partner at reading the conversation together today? Choose gold, silver or bronze.

Before you go

What other information would you like to know about where Anu and Manon live? How could you find that information?

5.4 What is your family heritage?

✓ **Research**
✓ Communication

1 **You are going to hear someone talk about where their family comes from. Prepare questions to ask the visitor.**

2 **Practise saying these phrases.**

That's very interesting!
That sounds nice/fun!
Sorry, can you repeat that please?
Excuse me but what does … mean?
Excuse me, can you explain why?

3 **Listen to your visitor talk about the place they come from. Ask your questions.**

4 **Make notes about your visitor.**

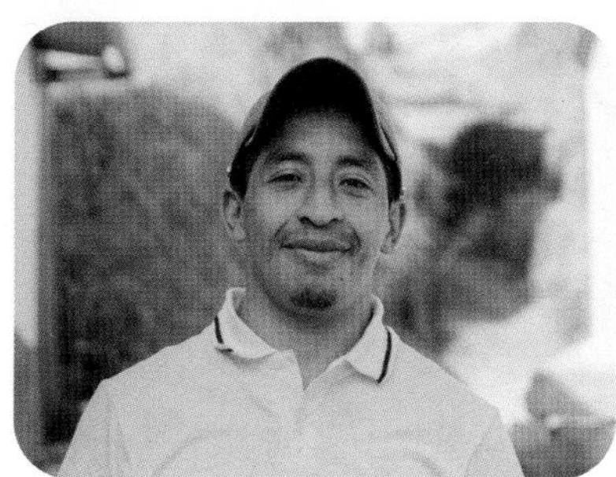

Talking point

Did you enjoy today's lesson? Did you learn anything new? Were you surprised by anything? Complete the reflection ticket on the worksheet.

Before you go

Why do you think our heritage is important? What happens if you lose your heritage?

5.5 What is it like starting at a new school?

✓ **Communication**
✓ Analysis

1 **Look at the cover of this book. What do you think the story is about?**

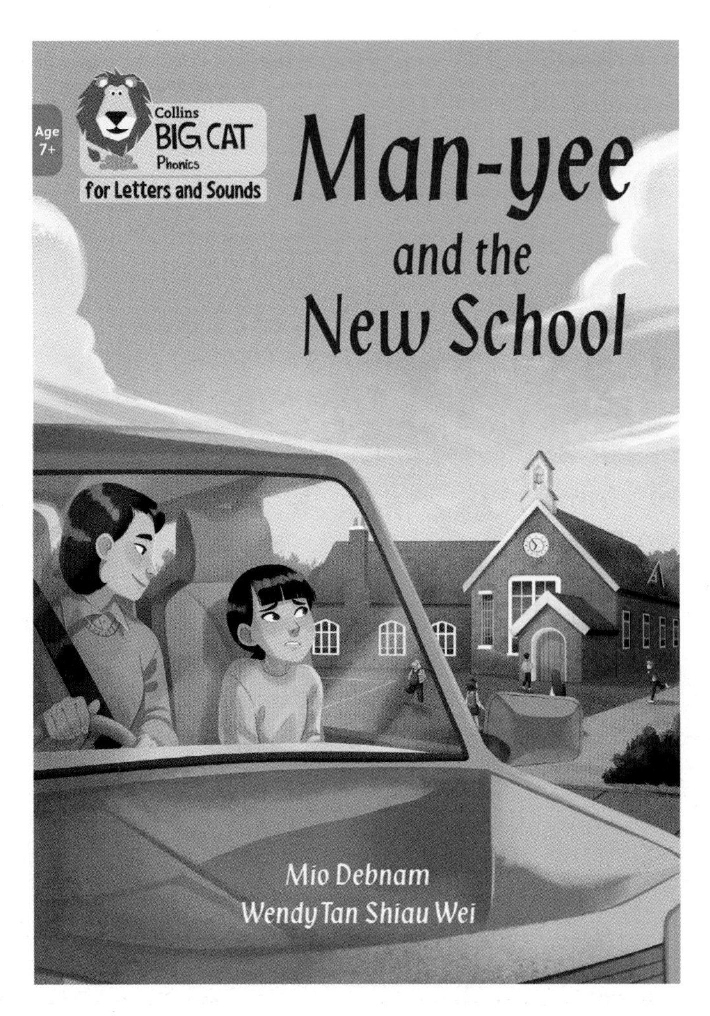

2 **Make a list of problems that someone moving to a different country might have at their new school.**

They might not know where to go.

3 **Look at the pictures from the story. What problems do you think Man-yee has at her new school?**

Useful language

I think that …

What do you think?

I agree/disagree because …

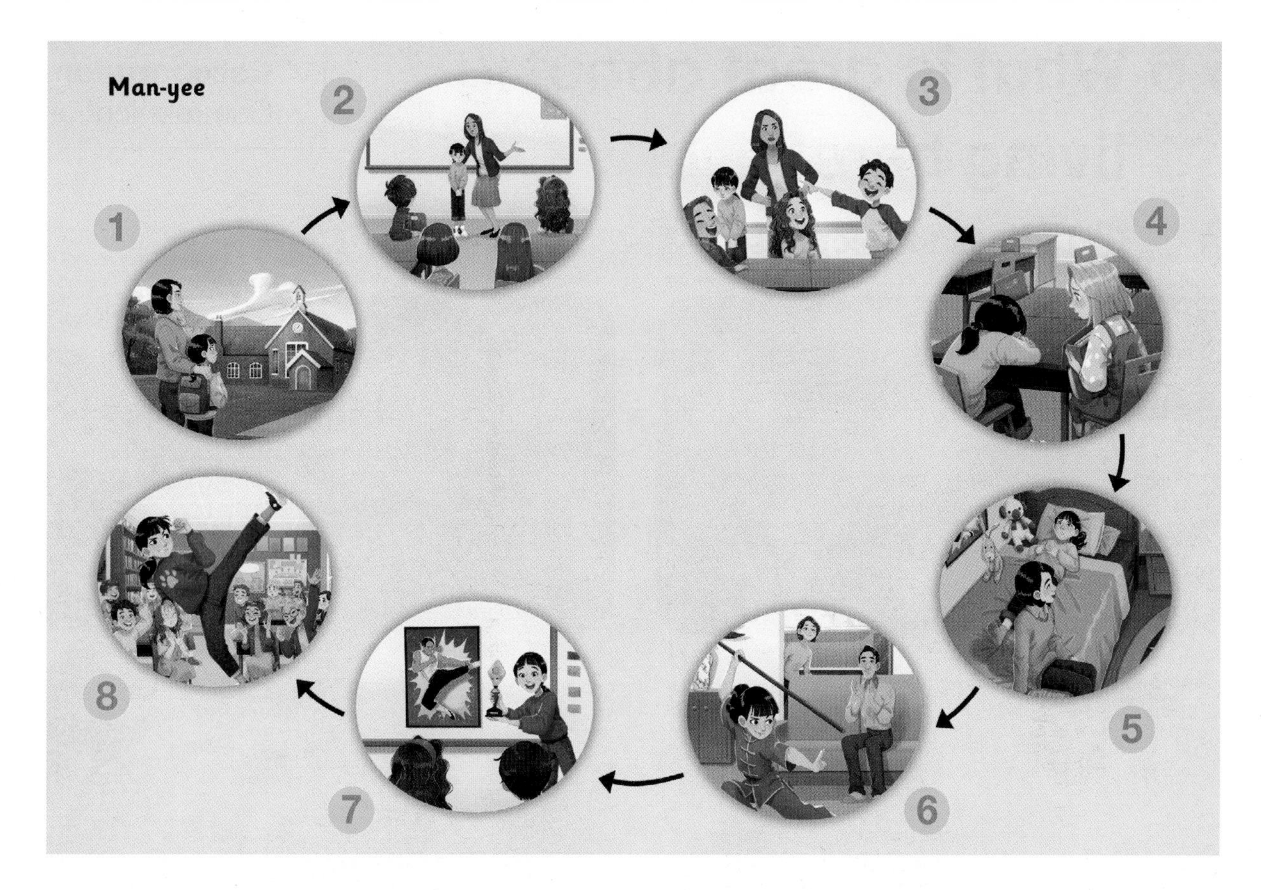

4 How does Man-yee get to know her new classmates? Is this a good idea? Explain your answer.

5 Listen to the story to check your ideas. Were you right?

6 Act it out!

a Act out picture 3 of the story.

b Act out the scene with the class being kind to Man-yee.

7 Imagine that you are starting at a new school like Man-yee. What could you show or tell your new classmates about yourself?

Talking point

How did these activities help you to learn more about moving to a new country?

Did you work well in a group today? Did you contribute ideas in today's discussions? Why, or why not?

Before you go

How do you think we treat new students at school here?

5.6 What is great about living here?

✓ **Collaboration**
✓ Communication

1 **Discuss the pictures.**

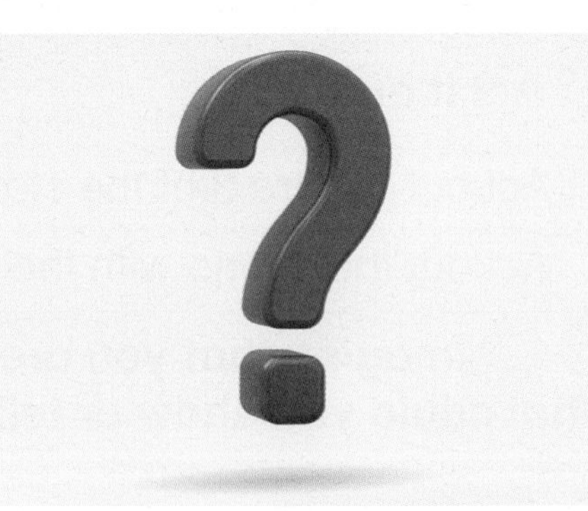

2 **You are going to make a poster to show what is good about where you live. Decide who will do what in your group.**

In your group, you will need:

- a leader
- a materials runner
- two writers
- two drawers

   **Make your poster. Use these tips to help you.**

Top tips

- Use pictures to show what you mean – remember, if someone doesn't speak the same language as you, they would find it hard to understand too many words.
- Write the title in big letters, very clearly, so everyone knows what your poster is about.
- Write lots of short texts rather than one big, long text.
- Check your spelling and grammar.
- Use colours and patterns to make your poster attractive – but don't overdo it or it will be confusing to look at.

4 **Present your poster to the class.**

Useful language

We'd like to show you our poster.

It shows what we think is great about …

We've included … because we think …

What do you think? What else would you add to our poster?

Do you have any questions?

Talking point

Did you like your role in the poster-making activity today? Why, or why not? What role would you like to try next time?

Do you think the posters would be useful for someone who is new to our area?

Before you go

What other ways could we tell someone what it is like to live here?

Unit 5 Final task: Make a welcome video

✓ **Communication**
✓ Collaboration
✓ Reflection

Read the final task and discuss the question.

Work in **teams** of five or six. **Make a video** to welcome a child from another country who is joining your class. **Write a script**. Decide how you will **present** your script, and who will **film** it.

1 What can you do to succeed in this task? Use the words in bold to help you.

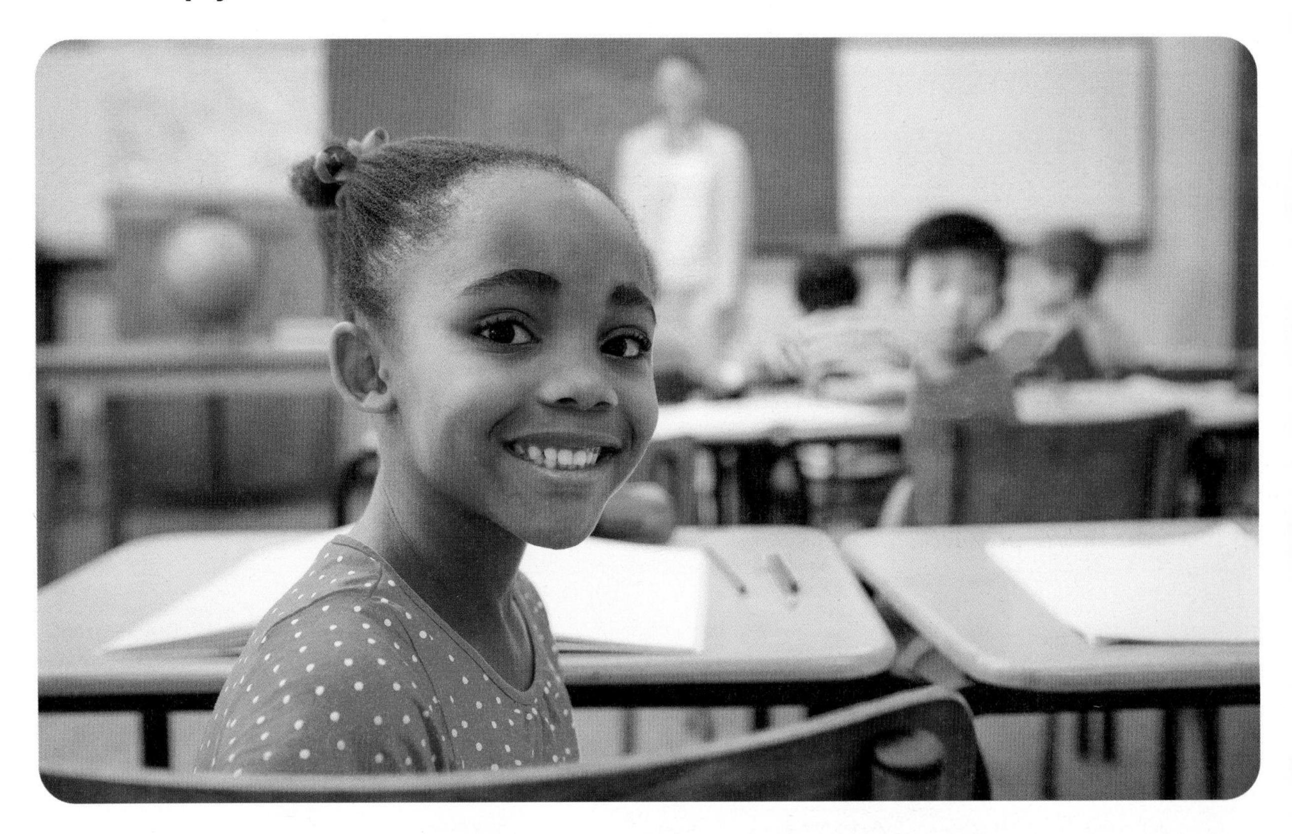

2 Read Genji's message and answer her question.

How do you think someone who has moved to where you live and is starting at your school might feel?

3 Read Anya's message and answer her questions.

How can you present information so that a new student will understand it? How can you make the new student feel welcome?

4 Make your video. Follow these steps.

- Discuss what you want to say and show in your video.
- Write a script.
- Practise reading the script aloud.
- Practise using the camera.
- Record your video.

Tips

- Use previous lessons in this unit to help you present your information clearly.
- Divide the roles and responsibilities.
- Use the task box success sentences to help you do the task well.
- Ask your teacher if you have questions.

5 Share your videos with the class.

Reflection: How successful was our welcome video?

a Complete the final task checklist. Use the worksheet.

Final task checklist			
Our video helps a person or people to understand about our class and to be happy in it.	☺	😐	☹
Our video clearly shows that we understand that we can make a positive difference to a new person joining our school.	☺	😐	☹
Everyone in our team can say what we did to improve our video.	☺	😐	☹

b Share your checklist with your team. Do you all agree?

c Take turns to say what you did to help the team. Do you all agree?

Before you go

Discuss these questions with your talking partner.

Did your group produce a video?
Were you happy with your video? Why, or why not?
What did you enjoy most about this task?
What did you find most difficult about this task?
Did your group disagree during the task? If yes, how did you solve the problem?

Glossary

closed question: a question where the person asked chooses one of several given answers 27

conclusion: a statement that is made after looking carefully at results 45

data: information or measurements 37

expatriate: person who lives outside the country where they were born 72

expert: a person who knows a lot about a topic 58

fact file: a way to record information about a place, a person or a thing 60

graph: a picture that shows information about sets of numbers or measurements 37

infographic: a text with pictures, numbers and symbols to help us understand information about a topic 37

open question: a question where the person asked can give any answer they want 27

pie chart: a circle divided into sections that show how much of the total each thing is 37

population: the number of people in a country or area 37

predict: think what will happen in the future 37

present: to show, tell or explain something to others 69

questionnaire: a set of questions created to find out what people think about a topic 26

survey: a way to find out information from a lot of different people by asking them all the same questions 2

tally chart: a way of showing how many times the same thing occurs 20

trade: buying and selling goods 56

Venn diagram: a way to show where two things are similar and where they are different 19

Acknowledgements

Every effort has been made to trace copyright holders and to obtain their permission for use of copyright material. The publishers will gladly receive any information enabling them to rectify any error or omission at first opportunity. The publishers would like to thank the following for permission to reproduce copyright material:

Cover and title page agefotostock / Alamy Stock Photo, p.1 ssuaphotos/Shutterstock, p.1 Didi Supriadi/Shutterstock, p.1 Henry Brink / Alamy Stock Photo, p.1 sandyman/Shutterstock, p.1 Salvador Aznar/Shutterstock, p.2 LeManna/ Shutterstock, p.2 Aisyah Az Zahra/Shutterstock, p.2 AfriPics.com / Alamy Stock Photo, p.3, 39, 55, 71 Elena Paletskaya/ Shutterstock, p.4 guruXOX/Shutterstock, p.5 wavebreakmedia/Shutterstock, p.5 Cultura Creative RF / Alamy Stock Photo, p.5 Igor Bulgarin/Shutterstock, p.5 Asia Images Group/Shutterstock, p.5 ANURAK PONGPATIMET/ Shutterstock, p.5 Kaew LIVER/Shutterstock, p.5 Irina Wilhauk/Shutterstock, p.5 stockpexel/Shutterstock, p.5 Berna Namoglu/Shutterstock, p.5 Riccardo Mayer/Shutterstock, p.5 NazArt/Shutterstock, p.6 *Dubai from the Sky* Text © Rob Alcraft, Illustration © HarperCollins*Publishers* Limited 2015, p.7 Prostock-studio/Shutterstock, p.7 Ebtikar/ Shutterstock, p.8 Phovoir/Shutterstock, p.8 Shine Nucha/Shutterstock, p.10 Ko Zatu/Shutterstock, p.10 Uldis Laganovskis/Shutterstock, p.10 a_v_d/Shutterstock, p.10 Hien Phung Thu/Shutterstock, p.10 ventdusud/Shutterstock, p.10 tilialucida/Shutterstock, p.10 Yingna Cai/Shutterstock, p.10 Nick Poon/Shutterstock, p.10 Ingus Kruklitis/ Shutterstock, p.10 Alfiya Safuanova/Shutterstock, p.10 GOLFX/Shutterstock, p.12 iadams/Shutterstock, p.12 Angela Davis/Shutterstock, p.12 Steve Cukrov/Shutterstock, p.12 Wirestock Creators/ Shutterstock, p.12 Click98/Shutterstock, p.12 Efired/Shutterstock, p.13 Happy_stocker/Shutterstock, p.14 Ramcreative/Shutterstock, p.14 StockSmartStart/ Shutterstock, p.15 Ground Picture/Shutterstock, p.15, 31 Rtimages/Shutterstock, p.17 Kartinkin77/Shutterstock, p.18, 24, 26, 27, 28, 52, 56, 62 Lopolo/Shutterstock, p.18, 26, 27, 29, 53, 63 Shyamalamuralinath/Shutterstock, p.19 raydignity/Shutterstock, p.20 Nataliia Zhekova/Shutterstock, p.21 Dmytro Zinkevych/Shutterstock, p.22 Aurelie Marrier d'Unienville / Alamy Stock Photo, p.22 Christian Nieke/Shutterstock, p.22 somchaiP/Shutterstock, p.22 vable/ Shutterstock, p.22 VanoVasaio/Shutterstock, p.25 WoodysPhotos / Alamy Stock Photo, p.25 DeiMosz/Shutterstock, p.25 good pixel/Shutterstock, p.25 Agarianna76/Shutterstock, p.25 Richard Johnson / Alamy Stock Photo, p.25 Viktor Kintop/Shutterstock, p.25 keith morris / Alamy Stock Photo, p.26 Inside Creative House/Shutterstock, p.27 ©HarperCollins*Publishers* 2020, p.28 antoniodiaz/Shutterstock, p.29 ChristianChan/Shutterstock, p.30 Efen Guy/ Shutterstock, p.30 Princess_Anmitsu/Shutterstock, p.30 Ben Schonewille/Shutterstock, p.30 Charlie856/Shutterstock, p.30 Iryna Tolmachova/Shutterstock, p.30 wavebreakmedia/Shutterstock, p.33 dieddin/Shutterstock, p.34 Zurijeta/ Shutterstock, p.34 mooinblack/Shutterstock, p.34 WESTOCK PRODUCTIONS/Shutterstock, p.34 belushi/Shutterstock, p.34 Drazen Zigic/Shutterstock, p.34 ESB Professional/Shutterstock, p.34 Art_Photo/Shutterstock, p.34 adriaticfoto/ Shutterstock, p.34 oneinchpunch/Shutterstock, p.34 Sabrina Bracher/Shutterstock, p.34–41, 44, 68, 70, 80 ShutterOK/ Shutterstock, p.35 John Batten – Beehive, p.35 *Six of Us* ©HarperCollins*Publishers* 2020, p.37 Sabrina Bracher/ Shutterstock, p.40 Maciej Czekajewski/Shutterstock, p.40 MBI / Alamy Stock Photo, p.40 S. Forster / Alamy Stock Photo, p.40 Damon Coulter / Alamy Stock Photo, p.40 REUTERS / Alamy Stock Photo, p.40 kitzzeh/ Alamy Stock Photo, p.40 Hero Images Inc. / Alamy Stock Photo, p.40 Damian Pankowiec/Shutterstock, p.40 Joseph Sohm/Shutterstock, p.40 Monkey Business Images/Shutterstock, p.41 wavebreakmedia/Shutterstock, p.42 Pixel-Shot/Shutterstock, p.43 Zurijeta/Shutterstock, p.44 FKVT/Shutterstock, p.44 Faizan qadeeri/Shutterstock, p.45 KadirKARA/Shutterstock, p.46 KadirKARA/Shutterstock, p.46 Vyacheslav Lopatin / Alamy Stock Photo, p.48 Davi Zapico/Shutterstock, p.48 StudioByTheSea/Shutterstock, p.48 Simon Annable/Shutterstock, p.48 Sabrina Bracher/Shutterstock, p.48 belushi/Shutterstock, p.48 Iryna Inshyna/Shutterstock, p.51 Aleksandr Simonov/Shutterstock, p.52, 53, 56, 62, 65 Hogan Imaging/Shutterstock, p.52 Pabkov/Shutterstock, p.53 addkm/Shutterstock, p.53 suprabhat/Shutterstock, p.54 f-stop1/Shutterstock, p.54 Oleh11/Shutterstock, p.54 Lufter/Shutterstock, p.54 Theeradech Sanin/Shutterstock, p.54 Galyna Andrushko/Shutterstock, p.54 Gcapture/Shutterstock, p.54 IHOR SULYATYTSKYY/Shutterstock, p.54 MERCURY studio/Shutterstock, p.55 MRAORAOR/Shutterstock, p.55 Bohbeh/Shutterstock, p.55 givaga/Shutterstock, p.55 Rita_Kochmarjova/Shutterstock, p.55 Amy Nichole Harris/Shutterstock, p.55 Song_about_summer/Shutterstock, p.58 Aedka Studio/Shutterstock, p.60 mijatmijatovic/Shutterstock, p.60 ixpert/Shutterstock, p.61 wavebreakmedia/ Shutterstock, p.62 Kir_S/Shutterstock, p.68 defotoberg/Shutterstock, p.69 Happy Art/Shutterstock, p.65 fizkes/ Shutterstock, p.67 Crazy nook/Shutterstock, p.68 New Africa/Shutterstock, p.68, 70, 71, 81 Paul Michael Hughes/ Shutterstock, p.69 Nikola Nikolovski / Alamy Stock Photo, p.69 Krakenimages.com/Shutterstock, p.69 SeventyFour/ Shutterstock, p.70 Ava Peattie/Shutterstock, p.70 Adam Dahlberg/Shutterstock, p.70 Mark Time Author/ Shutterstock, p.70 Attila JANDI/Shutterstock, p.70 Mogens Trolle/Shutterstock, pp.72–73 *Welcome to My City* ©HarperCollins*Publishers* 2017, p.74 Anas yacoub almaharmeh/Shutterstock, p.74 Catarina Belova/Shutterstock, p.75 Tirachard Kumtanom/Shutterstock, p.75 AJP/Shutterstock, p.75 AJR_photo/Shutterstock, p.75 Fernanda_Reyes/ Shutterstock, p.75 Prostock-studio/Shutterstock, pp.76–77 *Man-yee and the New School* ©HarperCollins*Publishers* 2021, p.78 GM Pictures/Shutterstock, p.78 Cacio Murilo/Shutterstock, p.78 Mark Thomas / Alamy Stock Photo, p.78 wavebreakmedia/Shutterstock, p.78 Dpeterson/Shutterstock, p.78 omravestudio/Shutterstock, p.79 3D character/Shutterstock, p.80 wavebreakmedia/Shutterstock, p.81 WESTOCK PRODUCTIONS/Shutterstock.